A Century
of
The
CENTURY

by
LINDA-MARIE DELLOFF   MARTIN E. MARTY
DEAN PEERMAN   JAMES M. WALL

WILLIAM B. EERDMANS PUBLISHING COMPANY
GRAND RAPIDS, MICHIGAN

This edition first published 1987 by Wm. B. Eerdmans Publishing Co.,
255 Jefferson Ave. SE, Grand Rapids, Mich. 49503

Library of Congress Cataloging-in-Publication Data

A Century of the Century.

1. Christian Century (Chicago, Ill.: 1902)
2. United States—Church history—19th century.
3. United States—Church history—20th century.
4. Liberalism (Religion)—United States—History—
19th century. 5. Liberalism (Religion)—United States—
History—20th century. I. Delloff, Linda-Marie.
BR1.C45 Suppl.   277.3'082   86-29243

ISBN 0-8028-0180-3

Contents

75497

Foreword

I do not propose to offer a miniseries to highlight the maxi-series presented in the following pages, where the editors of *The Christian Century* have ably condensed one hundred years of history into a relatively few pages of commentary on that history. Those who want the trends neatly laid out can do no better than to turn immediately to the succeeding pages in order to find a number of Ariadne's threads to guide them safely through the labyrinth.

Instead I will offer brief comments on some of the contributions to our thinking that emerge in reviewing an entire century (actually, about ninety years, if one accepts the strictures James Wall placed against including the decade of his editorship). We find here the cumulative guidance of Linda-Marie Delloff, Dean Peerman, Martin Marty, and James Wall, names familiar to all *Century* readers, dealing with the decades in that order. The first two are, as one of the four noted, "more narrative and fact-oriented," the latter two "more impression-istic and idea-oriented." All of which is as it should be, since the closer we get to the present, the more difficult it is to discern clear narrative lines rather than impressions, and the harder it is to know whether we yet have all the "facts" or are still proposing "ideas" for examination. No matter; variety is the spice of life at 407 S. Dearborn Street, Chicago.

Everybody at one time or another has gotten a laugh at the conviction of the early editors that they could denominate the upcoming hundred years as a "Christian century." One can at least retort that if the century failed to live up to that hope, it was hardly for lack of zeal on the part of the editors at the

Century. One is impressed, even overwhelmed—the quality of awe is invoked by one commentator—at the tenacity with which the editors kept looking at their world through the lenses of Christian faith, continually pointing out the places where the resultant focus still lacked clarity. They were sometimes wrong (a judgment easy to document in hindsight), but they seem to have made their own a healthy axiom by Karl Barth— hardly the *Century*'s favorite theologian: "Better something doubtful or overbold, and therefore in need of forgiveness, than nothing at all" (*Church Dogmatics*, IV/3, 2, p. 780).

A few things that emerge from scanning this hundred years of Christian history and journalistic reflection on that history:

1. One finds much evidence for the old adage that the more things change, the more they stay the same. If it is sometimes wearisome to experience déjà vu, it can also be encouraging; matters we think of as ominous in their newness and immensity turn out to have been on the scene before and seem thereby more manageable. In 1928, the editors of the *Century* were wondering why the United States should once again be seeking to impose its will on Nicaragua. Before the Catholic bishops' letter on the economy had even been thought of, the pages of the *Century* tingled with repeated examinations of the adequacy or inadequacy of capitalism to create enduring structures of justice. Those who face fundamentalism redivivus in their local situations will be heartened (or discouraged) by the reminder that this was a big issue throughout the 1920s, and that only the names and numbers of the players have changed. In a time when capital punishment is increasingly offered as a way to nip crime in the bud, the *Century*'s eighty-year war against such duplicitous reasoning furnishes material to continue the struggle. As a sophisticated McCarthyism in high places reasserts itself in the 1980s, it is important to remember that the *Century* took the lead in battling its cruder form in the 1950s. When the battle for Christian unity seems almost futile, strength to hang in there emerges when one follows the tortuous course of the ship *Oikoumene* through troubled waters and realizes that, many storms later, it is still afloat.

2. With all the ongoing similarities, there are also marked changes of perspective. Most apparent, perhaps, is the shift from the *Century*'s early days, when Protestantism was the quasi-official and almost unchallenged religion of the United States, to the present reality, in which, as the editors acknowledge, Protestantism can claim only to be "the distinctive faith of a creative minority." Protestantism is probably healthier for the cultural change it did not welcome. The present assurance that Roman Catholicism can be trusted not to subvert the nation's ideals has been increasingly validated, but the road to that conviction saw a lot of anti-Catholic debris scattered along the way. If, as I suspect, we have begun to see only the opening skirmishes of the intramural Roman Catholic battles of the next decade, we may witness the interesting spectacle of the *Century*'s editors taking sides in the struggle for a new kind of Catholicism rather than seeking to line up Protestants against Catholics.

In an unostentatious way, the *Century* was dealing with feminist issues far ahead of its time, not only in attitudes and in support of causes but also in such payoff matters as staff appointments—even though few women have yet contributed to the "How My Mind Has Changed" series.

3. On the matter of Christian approaches to war, surely the bottom-line item on the human agenda today, one can find almost any point of view and perspective one desires by reading enough pages of the *Century*. The ongoing concern for peace, so patent among all the editors, naturally receives ongoing attention. The journal has lived through a lot of wars since 1884, and attitudes have ranged from naïveté to disgust to anguish to outrage. One of the factors that made it hard for the *Century* editors to see the importance of U.S. involvement in World War II was their recognition, from the moment of its signing, that the Versailles treaty against Germany after World War I contained within it the seeds of a subsequent conflict. Why, they reasoned, should the Allies compound their guilt by participating in a war they themselves had made necessary? (It was the apparent isolationism of then editor Charles Clayton Morrison that led to a widely publicized rupture with Reinhold Niebuhr, and Niebuhr's decision to leave the *Century* pages

and found his own journal, *Christianity and Crisis*.) The advent of nuclear weapons made much of the earlier discussion of the pros and cons of modern warfare seem singularly out of date, and the *Century* has played an important role in the post-Hiroshima discussion, in which all the questions have had to be reformulated.

4. As the surveyors acknowledge on more than one occasion, the record on the most ghastly aspect of World War II, the treatment of the Jews, is far from satisfactory. Rather than assigning further blame or exculpation here, we can learn a few truths that were not so evident a generation ago: (a) there is no degradation of which the human heart is not capable, especially when aided by modern technology. So never say of atrocity reports, "Things couldn't be that bad, so we need not get involved"; (b) let treatment of Jews be the litmus test of the justice or injustice, the compassion or brutality, of any society or culture; (c) realize that if Jews need a place to go in flight from extermination, it is hardly responsive or responsible to suggest that they go anywhere they wish except the place where the speaker dwells; (d) in assessing who the Jews are, remember that there has been a lot of Jewish history since the writing of the last book of the canonical Hebrew Scriptures.

5. Another century looms. There is still a long way to go. Martin Marty can write of the late 1940s and early 1950s that "Protestant theology was in fairly good shape then." The implication is that it isn't in good shape today, and the implication can certainly survive serious challenge. Is there a recipe for a new theology? A preliminary version might go something like this: Take one world, a globeful of people, most of whom are victims; a handful of people passionately committed to justice; a God overseeing and supervising without usurping total control; an exemplary human life in which the globeful of people and the handful of people and the overseeing God are brought together so that the human life itself is transparent to the divine; a healthy respect for the past and a healthy skepticism about institutions that have an unhealthy respect for the past; human hearts in which anger and love are two sides

of the same coin; a willingness to risk judgments that might be wrong; and an ultimate optimism combined with a provisional pessimism. Mix well, and see what happens.

Such ingredients seem to me descriptive of the materials that *The Christian Century* has used during its first hundred years. Allowing for changed circumstances, they seem durable. If they can be maintained and built upon, maybe the next century can be a little better than its predecessor; not a "Christian century," surely, but a century in which *The Christian Century* will continue to play its critical and creative role.

ROBERT MCAFEE BROWN
Professor Emeritus of Theology and Ethics
Pacific School of Religion

A Century of
of
The
CENTURY

Charles Clayton Morrison: Shaping a Journal's Identity

LINDA-MARIE DELLOFF

A S WRITERS on religion in nineteenth-century America have emphasized, that era in our nation's history was one of undisputed Protestant hegemony. The country not only worshiped in Protestant churches, but embodied Protestant morals and mores in its social, cultural and political activities as well. Protestant clergy looked forward to the twentieth century with confidence, expecting to continue to assume positions of community leadership. The predominant mood of Protestantism at the turn of the century was positive, optimist and liberal—and its leaders welcomed the modernism heralded by the new age: the spirit of rationality and scientific inquiry, the growth of social awareness, and the sense of an expanding world. Protestant liberals were bent on proving that genuine Christian faith could live in mutual harmony with the modern developments in science, technology, immigration, communication and culture that were already under way.

This anticipatory mood is captured in one participant's narrative describing the renaming of a religious journal, *The Christian Oracle,* published beginning in 1884 by the Disciples of Christ denomination:

Dr. Delloff is managing editor of The Christian Century.

As the nineteenth century passed into the twentieth, the whole Christian world was in a mood of expectant optimism. The press was full of discussion and prediction of the wonders that would take place in the new era which the new century was ushering in. Dr. George A. Campbell, a Chicago pastor, was at that time editor of *The Oracle*. None of us liked that name. Campbell suggested that this new century must be made a *Christian* century. He accordingly proposed that *The Oracle* be re-Christened with that name. His friends . . . heartily agreed. And so in 1900 it was done. No name could have better symbolized the optimistic outlook of that period.

The writer of those words was a young Disciples minister, Charles Clayton Morrison, who in 1908 was to take over what was by then a publication floundering in financial distress, and eventually to turn it into the most influential Protestant magazine of its time.

When young Morrison completed high school in Jefferson, Iowa, in 1892, no one could have guessed that he would become a leader of his denomination and of liberal Protestantism in general. Indeed, he was a somewhat desultory student and had to do remedial work (especially in the classics) to qualify as a freshman at Disciples-related Drake University in Des Moines. It was not until several years later that he became a keen student with wide-ranging scholarly interests. However, he was already deeply involved in his faith and supported himself at Drake by preaching at a Disciples church in nearby Perry. He had no other immediate plans than to continue in his semirural pastorate near his family's home, but an unexpected call from the Monroe Street Christian Church in Chicago turned his course toward far broader horizons.

Morrison accepted the position at the small (less than half the size of the Perry congregation) west-side church in the city and became active in the Disciples community of the Hyde Park area located near the University of Chicago. There he continued his friendships with such distinguished Disciples leaders as Herbert L. Willett and Edward Scribner Ames, whom he had met when they came to Drake as guest lecturers. Willett, who taught at the University of Chicago Divinity School and who was later to become a controversial figure in the battle over the new "higher biblical criticism," was already an editor at *The Christian Century.* Morrison also became friendly with the group of men who had supported the journal since its move from Iowa to Chicago in 1891, and who were responsible for the 1900 name change. These included the most prominent Disciples in the city, though even collectively they had never been able to guide the magazine into solvency.

A FTER SERVING at the Monroe Street Church for several years, Morrison fulfilled a dream he had begun to develop when his intellectual sights had broadened during his last years at college: to embark on graduate study at the University of Chicago. However, as he recorded in his unpublished memoirs, "I chose the department of philosophy, rather than the Divinity School." The reason for this decision, he wrote, was that "I had a theory that the problems of theology originated in philosophy, and I wanted to get to the bottom of things." He continued in his description of those very important years of study.

> However dubious this theory may have been, I found myself confronting the ultimate issues of the nature of the world and the nature of man in a more naked form than I was likely to face them in theology. Besides, philosophy seemed to be the most exciting field in the academic world at that time. The head of the department was John Dewey, who . . . had gathered a faculty of his own disciples around him. Together they were elaborating a philosophical position which boldly challenged traditional modes of thinking and came to be called "The Chicago School" of philosophy. In addition to my courses with Dewey I studied with James Hayden Tufts in the history of philosophy, James R. Angell (later to become president of Yale) in psychology and George Herbert Mead in what might be called constructive philosophy.

It is probably fortunate that Morrison chose to study philosophy rather than theology at that time. His work at Chicago forced his naturally good mind to confront challenges and explore areas he might have avoided at the divinity school. It also made him permanently aware that religion must coexist with other aspects of human life and that its study must coexist with óther disciplines. It is evident that this period influenced Morrison's permanent interest in exploring the relationships between religion and its surrounding culture, with the result that a unique feature of the *Century* came to be its openness to articles on topics—political and literary, for instance—that did not commonly appear in religious publications. The full realization of these tendencies came later. At the time he left graduate school Morrison was, by his own admission, thoroughly steeped in Dewey's empiricism. Over the years he began to use that system as a foil for his increasing interest in theology.

After departing from the university, Morrison returned to the Monroe Street Church, where he ministered somewhat restlessly while the congregation and neighborhood changed with the large influx of immigrants. Since many of the newcomers to the neighborhood were not Protestants, his church was not growing and did not seem to have a strong sense of itself. When an opportunity for a new type of ministry presented itself, Morrison was quite willing to take a substantial risk.

> There was a small but reputable paper published in Chicago called *The Christian Century*. Though avowedly representing the Disciples of Christ, it had never gained a general circulation in the denomination, despite the high respect in which its succession of editors—four or five within the past decade—was held. I learned that it was about to suspend publication unless a mortgage of $1,500 was paid off. The holder of this mortgage saw that his only hope of getting his money was to find another editor naïve enough to imagine that he could make a go of it where a succession of editors had failed. This man was employed in the shop where the paper was printed. Evidently to try me out, he asked me to edit the paper temporarily. This I did for several weeks in that summer of 1908. By September, I had become fully intrigued, and when the sheriff's deputy arrived to sell the "property" on the block I bid $1,500 and became the owner.

At this time the magazine had 600 subscribers at $2.00 each. It was to be many years, and to require the help of many generous donors, before the *Century* finally achieved some financial stability.

At the time of the purchase, wrote Morrison later, "I had no other thought nor ambition than to keep the *Century* within

Charles Clayton Morrison,
editor of the Century *from 1908 to 1947*

the Disciples denomination, both as to its editorial outlook and its constituency. . . . For eight years or so the subjects we discussed and our news page were oriented by our interest in Disciples' affairs and problems."

By no means did this focus lead to smooth sailing during Morrison's first years in his new job; indeed, he was forced by the situation within his own denomination to alter his editorial philosophy—a development that eventually shaped the magazine's identity as a meeting ground and debating platform for controversial and opposing viewpoints.

Wrote the editor later in his memoirs:

> At the beginning, in my journalistic innocence of what lay ahead, I had planned an editorial policy that would minimize but not avoid controversial subjects. It was my intention to devote the major portion of my writing to themes in the general area of the "Christian life." . . . It was my desire that the *Christian Century* should transcend the controversial patterns that had long characterized Disciple journalism.

Times were difficult for the Disciples, who were split over several issues. At the beginning of Morrison's tenure, their most burning controversy involved the new higher criticism of the Bible, and much of the debate focused on Morrison's coeditor, Herbert L. Willett, an acknowledged champion of the new academic discipline. Because of Willett's controversial position, wrote Morrison, "another editor might have regarded him as a liability." But Morrison was devoted to both Willett and his views. The new magazine owner filled the *Century*'s pages with editorials supporting his colleague and attacking Willett's main detractor, the conservative *Christian Standard* (published in Cincinnati), the strongest and most widely circulated newspaper of the denomination at that time.

The controversy focused on whether Willett should be allowed to deliver a speech at the Disciples centennial gathering in 1909 in Pittsburgh. The *Christian Standard* argued No, calling Willett an "infidel" and a "betrayer of the Bible." The *Century* argued Yes and began to attack the *Standard* in strong language. Willett was eventually upheld, without any damage to his reputation; the controversy may even have enhanced it. As Morrison noted, "Willett's address was heard by the largest audience of the convention."

The higher criticism continued to be an important object of attention during the next several years, and the *Century* consistently supported its practitioners, publishing their articles and reviewing their books.

Another controversy had exploded at the 1909 convention and began to occupy much space in the magazine: the issue of "open membership." This debate concerned whether to accept as members of the denomination individuals who

Uneeda biscuits are often cited as an early example of a product whose market was developed solely by advertising. This ad appeared in a 1909 issue of the Century.

had not been baptized by immersion, the Disciples' practice. Over a period of more than four years, Morrison engaged in what he termed "a lover's quarrel with my denomination" over this issue. His editorials consistently supported accepting into membership such individuals without requiring them to be rebaptized by immersion, while many denominational leaders argued that this was a totally unacceptable practice. The seriousness of this concern to the Disciples permeates the relevant portions of Morrison's memoirs:

> It should be made clear to the reader of these pages that the Disciples had no ecclesiastical structure above the local church by which this or any other issue could be settled by authority. They represented on a national scale the concept of a town-meeting democracy. In such a body, the denominational newspapers exercised a far greater influence than in other denominations. They provided a kind of parliament for the discussion of questions of interest to the denomination. It was strictly in harmony with the Disciples' tradition for the *Christian Century* to direct the denomination's attention to a serious inconsistency in its practice and to an egregious error at a vital point in its traditional ideology. (1) The inconsistency was stated thus: The Disciples churches by requiring the rebaptism of members of other churches who apply for membership in a local church of Disciples deny their fundamental commitment to the cause of Christian unity. (2) The error in their thinking which had seemed to justify this sectarian practice was an egregious misconception of the meaning of baptism.
>
> We could not have touched a more sensitive nerve. The Disciples had spent more argumentative ingenuity in convincing others (and, as I believe, convincing themselves) that the New Testament meaning of baptism was immersion in water, than upon any other subject. Their firm conviction on this subject amounted to hardly less than a fixation or a stereotype.

The *Century* launched a series of twenty long editorials under the title "The Meaning of Baptism." In these Morrison challenged church father Alexander Campbell's rendering of the Greek word *baptizo* and his argument that made immersion identical with baptism. This controversy led inevitably to a debate over whether other churches are "true churches of Christ and whether the members of these churches are baptized members of the Church of Christ." To the *Century*, a negative answer to this question was theologically incorrect and came into conflict with the Disciples' highest ideal: Christian unity. Morrison had long supported the attainment of such unity, and he recognized the baptisms performed by all other Protestant denominations. He had also been the first Disciples of Christ minister to practice open membership.

This issue again brought the *Century* into conflict with the denomination's most influential papers—the *Christian Standard* and the newly conservative *Christian Evangelist,* formerly the publication of well-known liberal editor J. H. Garrison. However, the *Century* also received much support from its readers, and throughout the period Morrison printed many favorable letters on the topic. Eventually open membership became the accepted denominational stance.

Thus for the first five years of Morrison's tenure, the *Century* was a focus of controversy. Yet as a result of this period of strife, the editor and his journal both emerged stronger and more certainly headed toward the magazine's eventual transformation into a nondenominational publication.

D URING the years leading up to World War I the *Century* did address issues that reached beyond denominational boundaries. Many of these can be grouped under the general rubric of the social gospel, that movement having thoroughly captured the interest of editors Morrison and Willett. In addition to major articles by and about such figures as Washington Gladden, Walter Rauschenbusch and Jane Addams, the editors printed many pieces with titles like "The Social Gospel and its Relation to Home Mission Expansion" and "Humane Missionary Work at Ellis Island." They also ran a column titled "Social Survey," usually written by contributing editor Alva W. Taylor, which noted and discussed developments in such important areas as child labor, the growth of slums, and the obligations of churches for community outreach. Titles of some notices in the column include the following: "Eight Hour Day Movement in Britain," "Sanitary Dwellings in Austria," "Retirement Pensions," "Summer Vacation Schools," "Will the Theater be Redeemed?" Basically, the column writer reported on as many developments of (or impediments to) the social gospel movement as he could identify.

Walter Rauschenbusch (1861–1918)
RELIGIOUS NEWS SERVICE PHOTO

Another column, "The World is Growing Better," had a similar purpose but reflected even more of the magazine's optimistic liberal view of human and religious progress. In this space the editors carried items like "National Conference on Race Betterment," "Vocational Schools for Chicago," "Movie Censors Begin Work" and "British Fight Race Track Gambling."

During these years the magazine adopted the subtitle "A Constructive Weekly." The editors viewed their job as a committed ministry and believed that they were working toward building a positive society by calling attention to social evils and praising worthwhile social developments. One of the journal's more interesting features during this pre-World War I period was a column called "Modern Womanhood" written by the *Century*'s first female editor, Ida Withers Harrison. Her concerns included women's suffrage and the elements of making a decision on whether or not to work outside the home. In her innovative contributions she often profiled interesting

Women's suffrage demonstration
LIBRARY OF CONGRESS

women from various fields of endeavor, as in "A Tribute to Clara Barton" and "Women as Inventors." She also ran excerpts from the work of female writers—Zona Gale being frequently represented. Mrs. Harrison was a keen reviewer of books and plays which she identified as containing important social themes, especially those dealing with women.

From the first years of Morrison's term as editor, all of the staff members revealed a strong interest in the arts and their relation to religion. The magazine published fiction containing social gospel themes and ran a regular poetry column titled "Poems of the Social Awakening," carrying works by poets Edwin Markham, Vachel Lindsay (a Disciple from downstate Illinois—a particular favorite) and the *Century*'s own Thomas Curtis Clark. (It also published a great deal of poetry on other topics.) The journal ran articles on "the religious significance of poetry," and others with titles like "Shall Pastors Know Something About Art?" It published pieces by officials of Chicago's Art Institute, as well as articles by and on local sculptor Lorado Taft, in whose work Morrison saw portrayed "lofty ideas" and "the supremacy of the ethical."

Many of the books reviewed in the regular "Book World" column dealt with social issues, but the editors also included notices of academic theological monographs and of books on subjects not traditional for religious publications: literary criticism, philosophy and psychology. For example, books reviewed in the first months of 1910 included Herbert Croly's *The Promise of American Life; Education in the Far East*, by Charles F. Thwing; a philosophical study titled *Religion and the Modern Mind*, by Frank Carleton Doan; Jane Addams's *The Spirit of Youth and the City Streets; The Immigrant Tide*, by Edward Steiner; *Medical Inspectors of Schools* (a Russel Sage Foundation study); *A Modern City* (a scientific study of that phenomenon), by William Kirk; *The Leading Facts of American History*, by D. H. Montgomery; and Jack London's collection of short stories, *Lost Face*.

One important aspect of the editors' social concern was their concentration on a topic that would preoccupy them for many years: prohibition and the evils of liquor. Articles in this area carried such stirring titles as "Goliath Rum on the Run." The *Century* editors argued repeatedly that the use of liquor destroys social units—especially the family—and keeps people from realizing their natural potential.

In these prewar years the *Century* gradually turned its focus away from the Midwest and even began to include international coverage. Until 1914 the magazine's main global focus was on foreign missions and related topics. But in that year the editors began to write frequently about the war in Europe, publishing a series of editorials with the titles "God and War," "Prayer and the War," "The President and the War" and "Human Progress and the War." Though the position of the editors at this time was generally antiwar, it did not incorporate the pacifistic elements that were to characterize their post-World War I attitudes. Indeed, Morrison wrote in an editorial:

> There are some things better than life. There are some things gloriously worth dying for. There are some things gloriously worth giving your son for, and your husband and your father, and suffering for yourself in poverty and heart-break all the rest of your days. Truth and honor and the well being of others and the ideal of a better social order for future generations— these are all worth while for a man to lay down his life and for a woman to give up her husband or a mother to give up her son. To help establish these supreme moral goods is the great business of living, and if it takes life to establish them our humanity has always been heroically willing to give life without stint and without whining.
>
> It is not soft sentimentality, therefore, that moves us to deplore this present war. Our hearts revolt at it because there is no worthwhile moral issue at stake. It is a mad war, an irrational war, a hysterical and frenzied slaughter. And the thing wherein humanity suffers most is not in the mere shedding of blood, but the halting and inevitable turning back of those movements which during the long period of peace have been making for a new humanity, a new social order.

In other words, Morrison did allow that some wars could be worth fighting—but not this one. He deplored what he saw as useless bloodshed with no "supreme moral good" at stake. On the eve of developments that would lead to America's entry into the war, Morrison was speaking for a large segment of American Protestantism in his view that one of the greatest of this war's tragedies would be the destruction of social progress—a near-fatal blow to the social gospel. He was, of course, correct.

The years after the war were to see Morrison launch renewed efforts to reinvigorate the weakened movement. Meanwhile he supported Woodrow Wilson's conduct in foreign affairs and broadened the magazine's perspective on the areas in which those affairs were taking place.

At the same time—in 1916—he quietly relabeled *The Christian Century* "undenominational." ■

The *Century* in Transition
1916-1922

LINDA-MARIE DELLOFF

ROM the time it was established in 1884 in Des Moines, Iowa, *The Christian Century* had been published by and for members of the Disciples of Christ denomination. One day in 1916, as editor Charles Clayton Morrison was making his rounds through the magazine's southside Chicago office, he stopped at the desk of the employee in charge of subscriptions. He later recorded the experience in his unpublished memoirs:

> Glancing at the open mail before her, my eye caught the letterhead of Oberlin College. Picking up the letter I found that Henry Churchill King, president of Oberlin [a prominent Congregationalist], was renewing his subscription. This interested me. I took up the little sheaf of letters and looked at the signatures. To my surprise, I found that Lynn Harold Hough [a Methodist], then president of Northwestern University, was also renewing his subscription. What does this mean? I reflected. I asked the young lady to run off on the tape the entire subscription list (not a big job!) and give it to me. My eye went through the whole list to see if there were other non-Disciple readers of such prominence that I could recognize them. I found perhaps 20. If I can recognize 20, there must be many others whom I do not recognize by name.

This revelation set Morrison on a train of thought that was to have far-reaching consequences. Long an adherent of unity among the denominations, he was receptive to any developments that might seem to promote that goal. He decided

17

to try an experiment: in 1917 the magazine began to carry the subtitle "An Undenominational Journal of Religion." No announcement of the change was made; Morrison simply waited to see what the response would be.

Later he observed, "I knew that this subtitle was ambiguous. It would be interpreted by non-Disciples as we intended them to take it, and it could be interpreted by Disciples as implying the traditional claim that they were not a denomination. So the experiment was noncommittal."

Morrison needn't have worried about the reactions of his Disciples readers and financial backers—whose opinion concerned him profoundly since the journal still operated tenuously, almost from issue to issue. They were uniformly pleased with the change, which they seem to have understood immediately in the real sense which Morrison intended—i.e., interdenominational.

Morrison and his colleagues Herbert L. Willett and Thomas Curtis Clark (until 1924 the only full-time editor besides Morrison) began, as they put it, "unobtrusively" to expand the *Century*'s news department to cover events in other denominations. In several years, this resulted in the popular "News of the Christian World" department, for which the editors began to line up correspondents across the nation—and around the globe.

The new product met with success, and the subscription rolls began to increase. The editorial style and point of view were gradually oriented to a larger and more diverse public. As a result of the change, the editors felt that "the amenities which a denominational organ naturally observes toward other denominations were now less binding. We became almost as frank and open in expressing editorial opinion on the doings of Methodists, Baptists, Presbyterians, Episcopalians and others as we had always been on those of the Disciples."

In a few years—and after an advertising campaign in other publications—the journal had acquired roughly as many Congregational, as many Presbyterian, nearly as many Baptist, and twice as many Methodist subscribers as the subscription list of Disciples at the campaign's beginning. Smaller denominations were represented in proportion to their membership.

In a relatively short time, non-Disciple writers and editors began to appear with great frequency. For example, in the

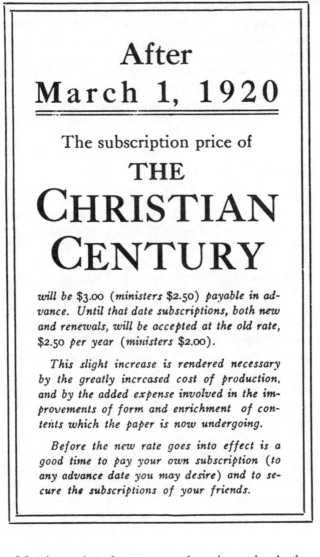

After
March 1, 1920

The subscription price of

THE
CHRISTIAN
CENTURY

will be $3.00 (ministers $2.50) payable in advance. Until that date subscriptions, both new and renewals, will be accepted at the old rate, $2.50 per year (ministers $2.00).

This slight increase is rendered necessary by the greatly increased cost of production, and by the added expense involved in the improvements of form and enrichment of contents which the paper is now undergoing.

Before the new rate goes into effect is a good time to pay your own subscription (to any advance date you may desire) and to secure the subscriptions of your friends.

teens Morrison signed on two columnists who both wrote nearly every week and who became immensely successful with readers. The first was Congregational minister William E. Barton from Oak Park, Illinois (who in 1911 had begun writing articles on the arts for the *Century*), whose pen name was Safed the Sage. Written in a formal, "antique" style, each of

19

his short pieces contained a moral point, often expressed in sharp-edged wit. In 1919, Lynn Harold Hough, whose renewal form had so influenced Morrison, began his column, "The Lion in his Den." Cast in a much more straightforward style than Barton's, yet often containing a veiled and ambiguous meaning, Hough's column provoked many letters to the editor. In addition to his column, he began to contribute regular articles on a wide variety of topics. (After leaving Northwestern, Hough had become pastor of a distinguished Methodist church in Detroit.) Also added to the staff was British Congregational minister Edward Shillito, who wrote a regular "British Table Talk" feature.

Several article series appearing in the magazine at the time indicate just how far Morrison was now able to reach for writers, both from other denominations and from the secular world. A 1921 series titled "Do the Teachings of Jesus Fit Our Times?" included authors Jane Addams, Joseph Ernest McAfee, Herbert Croly, Vida Scudder, Lloyd C. Douglas and Hough. Another series that year, "Some Living Masters of the Pulpit," profiled noted preachers of various denominations. For a 1922 series, "The Future of the Denominations," Morrison invited experts from a number of church bodies to comment on the situation of and prospects for their own groups. Frequent writers during the period included well-known adherents of various denominations: Harry Emerson Fosdick, Sherwood Eddy, Joseph Fort Newton, Joseph Ernest McAfee and John Haynes Holmes.

In their pursuit of church unity, the editors supported such cooperative ventures as the Interchurch World Movement, whose postwar object was "the careful survey of the fields and forces involved in the problems of world evangelization . . . and the avoidance of any duplication by various denominations." While recognizing that this was not "a fixed and final form of Christian unity," the editors applauded such cooperation.

A S THE *CENTURY* expanded its denominational horizons, it also increased its coverage of all types of religious movements. For example, while the editors had often lamented the growth of fundamentalism, in the late teens their attacks became more vociferous. They wrote pieces with titles like "No Time to Revive the Old Revivalism," in which they argued: "A wholesome evangelistic spirit is of the very essence of Christian experience and passion. But the very name evangelism has suffered through the perversions to which the fine art of soul saving has been subjected." Or, on another occasion: "The only trouble with the fundamentalists is that they have missed finding the fundamentals."

From 1916 into the 1920s, the *Century*'s main preoccupation, not surprisingly, was World War I and then its aftermath. While the editors were never enthusiastic about the possibility of U.S. participation in the conflict, when it became an inevitability they wasted no time in expressing their support for President Woodrow Wilson's decision. "War brings men duties," they wrote in April 1917, just after U.S. entry:

> America has not wanted war. We have deliberated while those who have become our allies have been fighting our battles. At last the most peace-loving president of America's history has been driven to declare for war. He is a Christian man. He has believed, as most of us believe, that though war is a mighty evil, there are some evils even worse.

While the editors supported participation, they did so in the spirit of Wilson's pronouncement that this was a "war to end all wars."

> It is our duty to hold to our hope of universal peace, even in the midst of war. . . . We may even now be taking the first step in the program of a League to Enforce Peace.

Even in the expression of such patriotic sentiments, one may discern hints of Morrison's later repudiation of armed conflict and his firsthand involvement in the Kellogg-Briand Peace Pact of 1928—a treaty designed to outlaw war. But at the beginning of America's entry into the Great War, the *Century* betrayed no signs of a pacifist impulse. In October 1917 the editors wrote the following:

> The pacifist who still thinks that his abstract "peace" is of more value than civilization itself is now a sorry figure. Horrible as Europe now is, more horrible would be the moral degradation and spiritual deadness of a world which would fall to the level of the present Prussian government.

As the war ended and the Treaty of Versailles was signed, the editors felt betrayed by a president whom they had formerly supported totally. The treaty, they believed, was harsh and unfair. It "looked to the past and sought punishment, when it should have looked to the future and sought reconciliation." They called the peace terms "unjust and vicious." Their feelings about the treaty strongly influenced their view of the proposed League of Nations. While they called the latter "the one saving feature of the Treaty," they expressed ambivalence about the concept because it was linked inextricably with that treaty.

Because of their increasing disillusionment with Wilson's leadership, the editors were not crushed by the results of the 1920 election. While acknowledging that it could be "a moment of great peril to the fine fabric of social idealism which has painfully been woven in the consciousness of modern Christianity," they chose to offer cautious support to the new Republican president, suggesting that they believed his promises to create some substitute for the League. "It is too easy to become cynical," they argued, predicting that the nation would soon emerge from its "emotional slump." They strove consciously always to maintain an open and optimistic attitude.

However, it took very little time for the *Century* writers to become thoroughly disillusioned with Harding, whom they saw to have quickly abandoned his promise not to let America resume an isolationist stance. In 1922 they were writing that "at the close of the war we left our international task half completed"—and the present administration had done nothing to achieve that completion. Further, the editors felt that the administration's handling of the war's domestic aftermath was deplorable. For example, even though they had supported the war and had chastised the pacifists, they had never condemned anyone's right to express any opinion whatsoever on the topic. So they were outraged by the treatment of objectors. In January 1922 a blistering editorial, "Political Prisoners and the Christian Conscience," summed up their views.

> The record of our attitude toward those who "for conscience' sake" refused to support the war is a matter which Christian intelligence can no longer decline to contemplate. We passed laws depriving such men of what they had supposed were their

constitutional rights of freedom of speech and press. We en-
forced those laws with a degree of passion in excess of that
obtaining in any other country, not excepting even Germany
itself.

And now the administration was still keeping many
protesters locked up—while the few it released were expected
to pay their own deportation costs. This the *Century* editors
regarded as intolerable. They were now writing frequent editorials with titles like "The Nation's Declining Moral Credit."

THE EDITORS' VIEWS on the postwar situation shared
attention with two other frequent themes: the need to re-
habilitate the social gospel—badly battered by the war—and
the necessity to impose prohibition and then to maintain its
enforcement.

The editors never wavered in their fierce advocacy of the
social gospel movement and felt its weakening to be one of
the war's great losses. They continued their pervasive coverage
of its developments and wrote frequent theoretical treatises on
its merits. Contributing editor Alva W. Taylor, an expert on
the topic, wrote major articles as well as a regular column on
the practice of social Christianity. During this period he paid
special attention to the rampant labor problems that the nation
was experiencing.

While the *Century* editors were generally prolabor, they
were not blindly so. For example, in 1917 they wrote editorials
condemning labor unions for discriminating against blacks. In
1919 they wrote of the labor movement: "Gone . . . for the
moment is its responsiveness to moral obligation. The way in
which organized labor tears up its solemn contracts without
scruple is one of the most ominous aspects of the present
situation." They also wrote other pieces expressing a balanced
view of the cooperation needed between labor and the capitalists. "It is no time for revenge," they asserted in 1921 after
a number of crippling strikes. "It is a time for understanding."

On other social issues of the day the editors were equally
forthright. For example, they were very vocal in their disap-
proval of capital punishment. "There is no evidence to show
that capital punishment is at all superior as a means of handling . . . criminals. It is cheaper, but it breaks down the very

thing that the community wants to build up, the sense of sanctity of human life."

The editors were similarly outspoken in condemning the racism that seemed to have become more virulent with the wartime influx of blacks into northern industrial cities. While frequently adopting a paternalistic attitude, the editors were sincere in their antiracist ideals. As ready to criticize such discrimination in the churches as elsewhere, they wrote in 1917, "Even in the Church of God there are still the remnants of this ugly and unreasoning hatred. . . . Men called bishops in the church of God [have] voted against having any fellowship in the church with black men." The editors also endorsed the woman's suffrage movement, writing, "There is no occasion for delaying further the ratification of the suffrage amendment. . . ." By its ratification, "an ancient wrong will be righted." They extended their demands for women's rights to the church as well, arguing in 1919, "It is inconceivable that there should be a world movement for a full franchise for women in politics without there being at the same time a movement for full opportunity for women in organized religion. The recent meeting in St. Louis of women preachers who propose to 'encourage capable and consecrated young women to take up the work of the ministry' is a significant sign of the times." This concern with prejudice against blacks or women was not pervasive among social gospel adherents, many of whom championed labor, for example, but had little to say about sexism or racism.

However, on the biggest social issue of the day—prohibition—almost all branches of the social gospel movement were in complete agreement, and the *Century* editors were among the most vocal, calling liquor the land's "worst menace." Having campaigned for prohibition since he assumed ownership of the *Century* in 1908, Morrison heated up his efforts as passage of the Volstead Act neared. There was no relenting after its passage, however, because of the widespread flouting of the act's provisions. Indeed, until long after repeal of the act in 1933, prohibition was one of the magazine's major preoccupations. The *Century* editors viewed the liquor industry as a corrupt, powerful cabal that exploited the worker mercilessly; they felt that the only way to solve the problem

Wet and Dry Map of Illinois

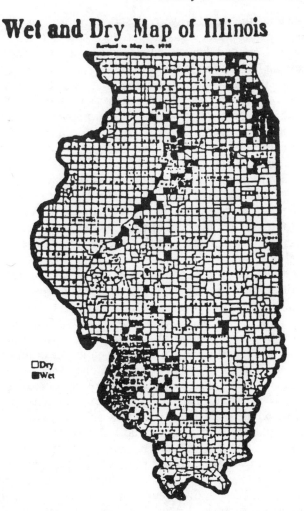

This township temperance guide appeared in the March 1, 1917, issue of the Century.

was to destroy the industry. (Interestingly, the labor unions of the day did not generally support the dry position.)

But the editors also maintained what today seems like a naïve psychological perspective, portraying liquor as the cause of degradation rather than emphasizing that poverty or oppression might lead to drinking. They were also naïve in believing

25

that once all the saloons were closed, former drinkers would suddenly display miraculously improved character.

Morrison and his colleagues were unprepared for the widespread lack of cooperation with the Volstead Act, but they marshaled their forces anew, arguing that with stricter enforcement it was possible to solve the nation's problems with "immoral personal behavior"—caused in large part, they thought, by liquor.

It is difficult to overestimate the importance of this issue for the *Century*. Woodrow Wilson's occasional seeming friendliness toward the liquor industry was one reason the editors began to suspect him. Similarly, after their mildly positive response to Harding's election, they subsequently perceived him as too soft on the wet forces. Such was the strength of their conviction on this issue that it strongly influenced their political allegiances.

By 1922 Morrison and his staff found themselves in the midst of several shifting tides. Their attitude toward the nation's moral rectitude was becoming more exhortatory, their attitude toward war more chastened. Late in the year they wrote of the recent conflict in Europe, "We may not be ready yet to say that we did the wrong thing in going in on the side of what we thought was democracy, decency and the rights of men. But . . . we now know that there is something monstrously wrong about that method of arriving at just ends."

Two points on which the editors did not waver were the centrality of social Christianity and the need for unity among the denominations. These were their most cherished goals. Toward both of these pursuits the editors maintained the relentlessly optimistic demeanor that characterized their liberal faith and their progressive view of life. They condemned pessimism at every turn. In the last issue of 1922 they were proclaiming a pox on "negation." "Building" is what they called for: "Our age awaits the era of the architect."

In the later 1920s and the 1930s Morrison and his colleagues were to prove themselves significant architects in a variety of liberal religious undertakings—not all of them solely journalistic.　■

Forward on Many Fronts: The *Century* 1923-1929

DEAN PEERMAN

"THE JAZZ AGE," "the Roaring Twenties," "Flaming Youth"—such phrases conjure up images of the 1920s as a carefree, frivolous, glamorous, prosperous time. But such nostalgia-influenced impressions are incomplete and misleading. True, it was the era of the flapper and the Charleston, of speakeasies and bathtub gin, of fads like Mah-Jongg and flagpole sitting, of the Ziegfeld Follies and Aimee Semple McPherson's revivalist follies, of baseball's phenomenal Babe Ruth, Hollywood's winsome Charlie Chaplin, aviation's heroic Charles Lindbergh, and pop psychology's positive-thinking Émile Coué (whose devotees twice daily intoned 20 times, "Day by day, in every way, I am getting better and better").

But it was also a period that saw much labor unrest, the Teapot Dome fraud scandal, a resurgent Ku Klux Klan, the Scopes "monkey" trial, the rise of Al Capone and the entrenchment of organized crime, the courtmartial of Billy Mitchell, the execution of Sacco and Vanzetti, and, at decade's end, the stock market crash. Events abroad included the advent of Mussolini's fascism in Italy, France's two-year occupation of Germany's Ruhr region, Mahatma Gandhi's ongoing nonviolent campaign to gain independence for India, the nationalist uprising in China, Stalin's victory over Trotsky for power

Mr. Peerman is a senior editor of The Christian Century.

in Russia, and Mexico's violent church-state conflict under the Calles government.

And America was changing, becoming increasingly industrialized and urbanized, and losing the cohesion and stability of an agrarian society. Although Warren G. Harding was elected president in 1920 under the slogan of "a return to normalcy," and although much of the country was still in thrall to its puritan-frontier past, there was no way that it could regain the relative tranquillity and innocence that had characterized its life in the years preceding World War I; "the war to end war," "the war to make the world safe for democracy," had been too traumatic, too thoroughly disillusioning. Underlying all that frenzied partying of the twenties there seemed to be a feeling of foreboding—a fear that another, more devastating war might be inescapable.

If America had lost much of its innocence, it had not lost its sense of hope and destiny. And certainly the pages of *The Christian Century* reflected high hopes for humankind during this period. No matter how trenchant the magazine's criticisms of the social order might be, or how acerbic its analysis of the ecclesiastical scene, it never despaired, never wavered in its conviction that both society and church were capable of reformation, even of redemption. The tensions and discontents of the times were looked upon as opportunities for the purposes of God. "It is the church alone that has the treasures of truth and divine grace in the gospel it proclaims and the Christ it seeks to interpret to an age of doubt and a world of sin. It is no time for hesitancy, depression or reaction. It is rather the inspiring moment of opportunity for unity and progress." So stated an eqitorial of December 27, 1923, commending the Federal Council of Churches (predecessor of the National Council of Churches) for its efforts to "unite rather than divide."

The *Century*'s editors did not want to "return to normalcy"—or to anything else. In fact, the magazine viewed President Harding's "return" mentality as paving the way for "moral fatigue" and the ensuing Teapot Dome oil-reserve conspiracy: "When the impulse of progress is displaced by the impulse of reaction a public atmosphere is generated in which corruption naturally thrives. . . . Whenever a nation or church imagines that its course is 'back to' anything, it has already given itself over to decay" (February 28, 1924). No, the only course for the Christian was forward—to build God's kingdom on earth. After a wartime hiatus, the social gospel and its proponents experienced a rejuvenation in the twenties, and more than any other journal *The Christian Century* was their mouthpiece. Describing the *Century* as "perhaps the most telling organ of the social gospel," historian Donald B. Meyer, in his book *The Protestant Search for Political Realism, 1919-1941* (University of California Press, 1960), asserts that "by the mid-1920's it ranked as the leading voice of liberal Protestantism."

C LEARLY, for Charles Clayton Morrison, having changed the *Century* from a Disciples of Christ magazine to a nondenominational one, virtually no subject was outside the purview of editorial and churchly concern, and the weekly journal dealt with many issues that the denominational publications rarely if ever confronted. Frequently it crusaded for causes long before the churches recognized their significance, and it sought to challenge church people to be the instruments of God's activity in the world.

An ardent champion of labor and the working person, the *Century* in the twenties advocated a constitutional amendment on child labor, a minimum wage, the abolition of the twelve-hour work day, and amnesty for incarcerated Wobblies (members of the radical Industrial Workers of the World who had been convicted of draft evasion, disruption of the war effort and the like). The magazine upheld workers' right to strike, even though the denominations and the Federal Council of Churches still regarded strikes as contrary to the method of cooperation and conciliation. But it also maintained that labor should not content itself merely with bread-and-butter matters, and it became increasingly scornful of what it saw as the AFL's bureaucratic conservatism: "The American Federation of Labor has become quite as orthodox as the church." The AFL lacked the moral passion and the moral stature to bring about the social revolution, the "era of industrial democracy," that the *Century* was calling for.

Although opposed to Marxist dogma and strongly committed to American democracy, the magazine was a critic of

Non-Employment in Heaven

(from the October 16, 1929, issue)

Lord, what will heaven be like,
That rich folks talk about?
To strut eternally
Before the down-and-out
Who never do find work
While walking streets of gold?
O Lord, for ice when hot,
Or heat, just once, when cold!
No land of rest for us,
Nor harps—a whistle, bell;
Lord, promise heaven has work,
Or leave us here in hell.

Elinor Lennen.

the country's economic system, especially laissez-faire capitalism—and nowhere more so than in the articles by frequent contributor Harry F. Ward, a professor of Christian ethics at New York's Union Theological Seminary and executive secretary of the Methodist Federation for Social Service ("Harry Ward is financed partly by Bolshevik money," accused one letter-writer). In Ward's view, the profit motive had succeeded war as a means of taking things away from others; it was a reincarnation of "our old friend the will to power."

It should frankly be acknowledged that the *Century* was sometimes more perceptive in its analysis than in its prescription. Recognizing the injustice of "the tremendous centralization of wealth and power in the hands of a few"—and that irresponsible power and privilege are "destructive of real brotherhood"—its solution to the problem was essentially an appeal to altruistic instincts, an exhortation to the privileged class to act sacrificially, to abdicate its privileges in the interest of "equality of opportunity and uncoerced cooperation" (November 18, 1926). Not many Wall Street tycoons or captains of industry were interested in responding to that kind of appeal.

A FERVENT defender of freedom of speech and the right of dissent, the *Century* condemned the blacklists issued in the twenties by the Daughters of the American Revolution and the American Legion. It fought the immigration law—signed by Harding's successor, Calvin Coolidge—which excluded the Japanese; it favored independence for the Philippines; in editorials with titles that could be repeated today—such as "What Are We In For in Nicaragua?" (January 12, 1928)—it opposed U.S. intervention in that Central American country. On both pragmatic and humanitarian grounds, the magazine was urging U.S. recognition of the Soviet Union years before that move actually came about—though it was careful to stress that recognition would not constitute approval. While generally supportive of the churches' missionary efforts, it was concerned that those efforts be free of any compromising ties to Western commercialism, colonialism and imperialism; it also emphasized the importance of developing indigenous Christian leadership in mission lands.

A much-debated issue in the *Century*'s pages was the situation of the American and European missionaries caught up in China's civil chaos of the mid-twenties; their lives were endangered, and a few of them, perceived as hostile to the nationalist cause, were killed. Paul Hutchinson, who prior to becoming managing editor of the *Century* in 1924 had served for several years as a Methodist missionary in China, concluded a 1927 series of background articles on that country by saying that "America has come to be lumped with those nations whose primary interest in China is the securing of settled markets, whether for the winning of dollars or the winning of souls." Speaking with prescience, the journal warned that the West's arrogant conduct toward China—unequal treaties, gunboat protection of missionaries, and so on—might force that country into the communist camp.

Of the three major international Christian conferences of the 1920s—Stockholm 1925 (Life and Work), Lausanne 1927 (Faith and Order) and Jerusalem 1928 (International Missionary Council)—the latter found the greatest favor with *Century* editors, in part because one of its resolutions stated that the use or threat of armed forces to protect the missionary and missionary property "not only creates widespread misunderstanding as to the underlying motive of missionary work, but also gravely hinders the acceptance of the Christian message," and went on to urge mission societies to "make no claim on their governments for the armed defense of their missionaries and their property." (The Stockholm conference was described by the magazine as impressive in its composition but given over to "platitudinous garrulities"; Lausanne was "an ugly picture"—a unity conference at which doctrinal differences prevented the participants from coming together at the Lord's Table.)

On the domestic civil rights scene of the twenties, the *Century,* though uneasy about the possible social consequences of the large influx of blacks from the South to the North, pleaded for just treatment of the black migrants. Equality was the watchword—equal opportunities for education, equal political rights, equal justice before the courts, equal pay for equal work. The magazine campaigned for the admission of blacks to labor unions and called for a federal antilynching law; it denounced Jim Crow laws and excoriated the night-riding Ku Klux Klan, whose membership reached 4 million early in the decade.

In *American Protestantism and Social Issues, 1919-1939* (University of North Carolina Press, 1958), Robert Moats Miller speaks of the *Century* as displaying in this period "a sensitivity toward the Negro probably unmatched in any paper in the country, religious or secular." But while holding high the banner of equality, on the matter of social integration the journal occasionally succumbed to the separate-but-equal fallacy. For example, when white students at a high school in Gary, Indiana, in 1927 went on strike to protest the enrollment of twenty-four blacks, the *Century* deplored the white students' action but went along with Indiana's segregated-school solution—even though granting that such a solution might not be ideal "either socially or morally" and surely was not ideal "from the standpoint of a religion which would wipe out all racial barriers." It then went on to say: "Such an adjustment the majority of Negroes are willing to accept. By their acceptance they show their patience and their wisdom" (October 13,

1927). With this comment the magazine perhaps reached its
nadir on the subject of race relations.

T HE CONTROVERSY between modernists and fundamentalists was going full tilt during the 1920s, and the
Century was in the forefront of the fray. The fundamentalists
were responding to what they saw as a crisis of belief, and in
their view that crisis was occasioned not only by the attacks
on orthodoxy coming from Darwinists, empiricists, agnostics
and the like, but also by the "heretical" teachings of theological liberals and biblical scholars. For them, anyone who did
not subscribe to the five "fundamentals"—the plenary inspi-
ration and inerrancy of the Bible, the virgin birth of Christ,
the substitutionary blood atonement, the bodily resurrection
and the Second Coming—was beyond the pale. By mid-decade the movement claimed one-fourth of the population as
adherents, and it was able to gather overflow crowds into Car-
negie Hall to hear harangues against evolution.

In doing battle with fundamentalists, the *Century* sometimes dismissed them with disdain: "The fundamentalists are
a weak imitation of the Ku Klux Klan. . . . America dare not
laugh at the [Klan] very heartily any longer for it has become
too big and sinister, but the fundamentalists are a big joke"
(October 11, 1923). At other times it counseled "tolerance for
the intolerant," on the ground that a person may hold a very
bad theology and still be "a Christian worthy of all love and
fellowship." Moreover: "Every liberal group that wants to
maintain its right to the name ought to make sure that it is
liberal enough to make a place within it for conservatives"
(July 5, 1923). But the journal was consistent in its conviction
that the fundamentalists' fundamentals were not Jesus' fundamentals, that in preaching a gospel about Jesus they were
forsaking the gospel *of* Jesus. "To the fundamentalist love is
an *attribute* of God. To the modernist love is the very *essence*
of God" (March 20, 1924).

The Baptists and the Presbyterians were especially af-
fected by the fundamentalist revival, and for a time militant
fundamentalists gained the ascendancy in both groups. A favorite target of the heresy hunters among them was Harry

A Klan march in St. Petersburg, Florida, about 1926
KEYSTONE-MAST COLLECTION, UNIVERSITY OF CALIFORNIA, RIVERSIDE

Emerson Fosdick, noted preacher at New York's First Presbyterian Church, a professor of homiletics at Union Seminary,
and a frequent *Century* contributor. Because he was a Baptist
occupying a Presbyterian pulpit, for a time it was difficult for
the diehards of either group to get at him. But eventually he
was compelled to resign after refusing to subscribe to the
Westminster Confession. Commented the *Century*: "The spirit
of the inquisition is among us. We do not use its apparatus,
but its presuppositions and its consequences still operate. The
sacrifice of the most conspicuously successful ministry in
America to the assumptions of creedal and ecclesiastical con-
formity is a commentary on the character of our religion which
should make the whole church blush" (October 16, 1924).
Fosdick's career went forward, however, culminating in his
long tenure at New York's Riverside Church.

In the summer of 1925 the fundamentalist-modernist
controversy reached something of a climax in the trial of
John T. Scopes, a high school biology instructor in Dayton,
Tennessee, who had defied the state's new law against the
teaching of evolutionary theory. For the fundamentalists, the
concept of evolution was demeaning to humanity; they called
its defenders "baboon boosters." They also felt—as do today's
creationists—that evolution was contrary to biblical truth. In
the *Century*'s view, evolution was simply God's way of working
in the world. But as for the trial in Dayton, the magazine
accurately predicted that it would be "foolishly sensational"
rather than substantive, with attention focused on the verbal
sparring of two renowned orators: the agnostic Clarence Dar-
row, attorney for the defense, and the fundamentalist William
Jennings Bryan, expert witness for the prosecution. "Booming
medievalism" and "amateur dramatics" were among the journal's terms for the proceedings.

Bryan, the Great Commoner, was a major disappointment to the *Century*. Secretary of state under Woodrow Wilson
and an old-line progressive, he had been touted by the magazine as a valiant crusader for peace, women's suffrage, regulation of business and other worthy causes; now, unfortunately,
the old idealist had become captive to obscurantism and reaction, wreaking havoc within the Presbyterian fold and spout-
ing such pitiful slogans as "You believe in the age of rocks;

I believe in the Rock of Ages." He died five days after the Dayton trial ended, becoming a martyr in the view of his admirers among the faithful. His influence lingered for a time, but as the decade wore on, the fundamentalist furor simmered down. Not that the modernists could claim victory; a relative peace, or at least a truce, was achieved because moderates and "tolerationists" on both sides prevailed, with hard-core fundamentalists breaking away from mainline denominations to form their own flocks.

ON ONE ISSUE, however, many religious liberals and conservatives did concur in the twenties—and that was national prohibition. Although morals, manners and customs were undergoing drastic changes during the decade, by and large the *Century*'s editors accepted such changes as inevitable. Occasionally they did call for, say, a clean-up of the movies (though stopping short of a demand for legal censorship). But they gave scant heed to such minor matters as women's dress styles, dancing and card playing; indeed, they defended the validity of play and leisure pursuits—even on Sunday, if that were the only time available. An advocate of sex education in high schools, the paper tended to be sympathetic toward young people. "Flaming youth" flames, it said, "because their elders pile combustible material around them and supply the torch" (May 19, 1927).

But the liquor traffic was something else altogether. In the eyes of the *Century,* it was an unmitigated evil, and drinking was not simply a matter of personal morality but a social problem akin to that of slavery in the previous century. With the enactment in 1919 of the Eighteenth Amendment to the Constitution and the Volstead Act as the instrument of implementation, for a time the fight to abolish the saloon seemed to have been won. To the *Century,* the prohibition amendment was "the most constructive and necessary piece of legislation that has been enacted since the declaration of independence was signed" (October 18, 1923), and contributing editor Alva W. Taylor erroneously prophesied that "a new generation is growing up that will never know John Barleycorn except in history" (March 8, 1923) and that the Eighteenth Amendment "will never be repealed" (July 12, 1923).

Like many prohibitionists, the editors underestimated the opposition. Enforcement became more and more difficult; lax or nonexistent in some areas, it was underfunded everywhere, and bootlegging and smuggling reached virtually uncontrollable proportions. Inevitably, the drys differed among themselves about ways to prevent "nullification of the Constitution." The *Century,* for example, was often at odds with the church-sponsored Anti-Saloon League, which had been the driving force behind prohibition; one of its chief complaints was that the league supported "political drys"—candidates who, however unsuitable or unsavory they might be otherwise, were deemed acceptable simply for taking a dry stand.

Coolidge, like Harding before him, proved to be less than wholehearted about enforcement of the Eighteenth Amendment, and in this instance the *Century* regarded the silence of "Silent Cal" as "no excusable idiosyncrasy" but "a refuge under which law-breakers hide" (July 1, 1926). So when the election of 1928 came around, the journal welcomed it as a clear-cut national referendum on prohibition—the dry Herbert Hoover versus the very wet Al Smith. On some issues—foreign policy, big business, tariffs—the editors found Smith, a man of "candor and courage," to be more congenial, more liberal, than Hoover. But to them the destructive role of liquor in modern society was the paramount liberal issue. Lukewarm endorsement of the dry Hoover; praise for but non-support of the wet Smith—this circumstance, said some readers, laid the *Century* open to the same charge of single-mindedness that it had leveled at the Anti-Saloon League.

But Al Smith was also a Roman Catholic, and for *Century* editors that was another reason to question his candidacy. They did so in rather restrained fashion, but they did so nonetheless:

> As a form or system of worship [Roman Catholicism] raises no legitimate or relevant question in any enlightened American's mind as to the presidential candidacy of one who professes it. But as a form or system of government it raises a profoundly legitimate and relevant question concerning the fitness of any presidential candidate who owns allegiance to it. Catholicism as a form of government comes into clash with American institutions in several definite areas of conflict such

Al Smith campaigning in 1928
MUSEUM OF THE CITY OF NEW YORK

as marriage, education, and property, in addition to its clash with the fundamental American principle of the relation of church and state [November 1, 1928].

Reinhold Niebuhr, who had first begun writing for the *Century* in 1923 and who had become a contributing editor in 1925, took exception to the magazine's stance on Smith. In a letter he granted that that stance was "of different quality from that taken by protestant bigots," but he also doubted "whether the position is well taken because it does not allow sufficiently for the change in temper and policy which the atmosphere of a protestant country forces upon papal politics. An organization is never as uniform or as united as its official pronouncements would lead one to suppose" (September 13, 1928). (Niebuhr himself supported neither Smith nor Hoover, but the socialist Norman Thomas.) As early as 1924, incidentally, Niebuhr was making statements about Catholicism that were more favorable than was generally the case in the *Century*'s pages: "Both the Catholic and Anglican churches have better records for courage on social and economic issues than congregationally organized communities in which the individual prophet is frequently at the mercy of a congregation which may contain many men who do not want religion to 'interfere with business' " (December 25, 1924). In that preecumenical era, however, most of the magazine's editors and writers could not seem to forget such edicts as Pope Pius IX's Syllabus of Errors, which condemned modernism, democracy, church-state separation and freedom of religion.

CHURCH UNITY continued to be a central *Century* emphasis in the twenties. Envisioning the true church as a democratic brotherhood shorn of "sterile dogma" and dedicated to service—to knowing and living "Christ's religion of goodwill and of unselfish righteousness and love"—the magazine tended to equate denominationalism with narrow sectarianism. "There is no place for denominational religion in a democratic society," it declared; "in the degree in which [denominational] 'rights' and prerogatives are assured, in that degree will religion and all the social processes to which it is vital go from bad to worse" (February 8, 1923). Denominational divisions were a hindrance to any effective relationship between public-minded religion and the actual policies of the social order: "Each sect is shut up in its own compartment. . . . The Christian opinion of the nation is fused only with greatest difficulty and only under stress of fearful crises. It is the wretched denominationalism of our Christianity that is responsible for this impotence" (November 15, 1923).

When Episcopalians in New York went outside the fold in search of funds for the building of St. John the Divine, the magazine maintained that a cathedral—even a "medieval" one—built with interfaith money should have an interfaith ministry. In 1925 it applauded John D. Rockefeller, Jr., for offering to donate $500,000 to the building fund on the condition that some non-Episcopal Christians be named to the cathedral's board of trustees. The offer was turned down by the bishop, and the *Century* accused him of quenching the Holy Spirit (February 19, 1925). St. John the Divine was being promoted as a democratic and community center of worship— "a house of prayer for all people," in the words of the bishop—but to the magazine it was "a denominational church, and a very narrow denominational church at that . . . only costing more than most denominational churches cost" (April 2, 1925).

That same year, 1925, saw the formation of the United Church of Canada, which brought together Methodists, Congregationalists and Presbyterians. Although the *Century* was not always precise about what should replace the "old and decadent scheme of meaningless separation," it certainly looked upon the Canadian event— "the first large-scale achievement of organic union of separate denominational families since the protestant reformation"—as a monumental step in the right direction. Editor Charles Clayton Morrison was on hand for the consummation service in Toronto, which he later characterized as a "pentecostal experience."

Morrison never lost his fervor for church unity, but ultimately he did temper his anticreedal, ultracongregationalist posture, acknowledging that he had undervalued history and tradition, had relied too heavily on empiricism and was guilty of a degree of reductionism. In a revealing retrospective article he stated:

> By the end of the 1920's, I was beginning to be conscious of the discrepancy between my two loyalties—my instinctive loyalty to my Christian inheritance and my intellectual loyalty to an empirical method of thought. I had baptized the whole Christian tradition in the waters of psychological empiricism, and was vaguely awaking to the fact that, after this procedure, what I had left was hardly more than a moralistic ghost of the

distinctive Christian reality. It was as if the baptismal waters
of the empirical stream had been mixed with some acid which
ate away the historical significance, the objectivity and the
particularity of the Christian revelation, and left me in complete subjectivity to work out my own salvation in terms of
social service and an "integrated personality" [November 8,
1939].

OVERRIDING all other *Century* concerns in the twenties,
however, was the quest for peace and a warless world.
Scarcely a week went by in which the paper did not have at
least one editorial, article or report dealing with the peace
movement. Although editor Morrison did not espouse a tho-
roughgoing pacifism—as did such frequent *Century* writers as
Sherwood Eddy, Kirby Page and Devere Allen—he nonetheless looked upon pacifists as "true patriots." It was his conviction that the church should declare that it would never again
use the "ecclesiastical function" in support of war, and in this
period he argued that the denominations should get out of the
military chaplaincy business.

When a split developed in the ranks of the peacemakers
about whether the United States should enter the League of
Nations, the *Century* eventually sided with those who opposed
entry, viewing the organization as too bound up with the ig-
nominiously unfair Treaty of Versailles; dependent on military
sanctions, it was "a league to enforce peace by the use of war
itself" (January 26, 1928).

While World War I was still under way, Salmon O. Levinson, an energetic, public-spirited Chicago corporation law-
yer, began to investigate the standing of war in international
law and discovered, to his astonishment, that not only was
there no law against war, but that war was indeed the supreme
legality in international relationships. How can we abolish war
so long as it is legal to wage war? So Levinson asked in the
New Republic of March 8, 1918, and from that small beginning grew a movement that culminated a decade later in the
Kellogg-Briand Pact (officially, the Pact of Paris). By 1924
The Christian Century was an enthusiastic participant in Levinson's crusade to outlaw war; in a signed piece Morrison
wrote: "The problem of ridding the world of war is the simple
problem, primarily, of making war a crime, of de-legalizing

it, of reducing it from its present status of right and respectability and honor to that of outlaw" (April 10, 1924). Levinson and Morrison became personal friends as well as co-crusaders.

The road to ratification of Levinson's proposal was to take many twists and turns, but eventually the idea of abolishing the institution of war caught on with the general public. So when in June of 1927 France's foreign minister, Aristide Briand, proposed a nonaggression treaty between his country and the United States, Frank B. Kellogg, Coolidge's secretary of state, countered with the suggestion that the treaty should be a multilateral, not just bilateral, pact against war—and to the *Century* the announcement of this U.S. peace policy was nothing less than "the most important event in modern history" (January 19, 1928). Prolonged negotiations ensued, consisting primarily of Kellogg's efforts to keep the treaty free of qualifications that would weaken it.

Fifteen nations signed the Kellogg-Briand Pact in Paris on August 27, 1928; before long virtually every sovereign nation in the world had joined in. Charles Clayton Morrison was on hand for the Paris signing; it was shortly before the twentieth anniversary of his editorship of the *Century,* and no anniversary gift could have brought him more joy. "An incredible event," he called it, "a consummate hour." And letting his exuberance get away from him, he wrote in italicized hyperbole: *"Today international war was banished from civilization"* (September 6, 1928). On January 15, 1929, the U.S. Senate ratified the pact with only one dissenting vote. At the time Morrison stated that the treaty was "absolute, water-tight, bullet-proof . . . [with] not a single loophole in it." But it was not followed up with what he called "the other side of outlawry": an adequate mechanism of peace. The pact never really counted for much, although it was employed successfully in resolving a China-U.S.S.R. dispute in 1929, and its principle was invoked by Justice Robert Jackson as a procedural basis for the Nuremberg war-crimes trials after World War II.

With the advantage of hindsight, it is easy to say that the visionary peacemakers of the twenties were overly optimistic, very naïve, much too trusting. But they were at least right in predicting that a second world war would be far worse than the first. A *Century* editorial of June 4, 1925, reads: "In the outlawing of war it is the plighted word of the nations that is our ultimate support. If that fails, civilization has come to something like a cosmic jumping-off place." In the years that followed the Pact of Paris, "the plighted word of the nations" seemed a frail reed indeed—as the world edged closer to that "cosmic jumping-off place." ■

Breadlines and
Storm Clouds:
The *Century* 1930-1937

DEAN PEERMAN

W HEN THE stock market crashed in October of 1929, *The Christian Century* was not unduly distressed; in fact, it viewed what had happened on Wall Street as potentially salutary, offering the American public "the privilege of sobering up" after a two-year "speculative debauch." But the *Century* was hardly alone in thinking that the crash could teach a much-needed lesson; such public figures as President Herbert Hoover, former President Calvin Coolidge, John Maynard Keynes and Henry Ford thought so, too. The gloomiest forecasters predicted nothing more than a recession, to be followed by a sharp upturn within a few months. The *New York Times* did not even pick the market collapse as the top story of 1929, instead choosirg Richard Byrd's South Pole expedition. In January 1930, Andrew Mellon, secretary of the treasury, "could see nothing that is either menacing or warranting pessimism"; Hoover announced in May that "we have now passed the worst"; in September the president of the New York Stock Exchange, Richard Whitney, declared that "the business horizon is clear." But by then several million people were out of work and banks were failing all over the country, and by 1933—in the depths of the Great Depression—the number of unemployed had reached 16 million, or about one-third of the available work force.

As the depression deepened and human suffering on a massive scale ensued, it became increasingly evident that the nation was in the grip of a grave economic and social crisis—one that would not soon abate. In a memorable account epitomizing that crisis, *Century* managing editor Paul Hutchinson described a demonstration in which 20,000 men marched in pouring rain through Chicago's downtown area shouting, "We want food!"; they then assembled on the lakefront for a mass meeting in which they stood ankle-deep in mud (November 9, 1932).

In the opinion of the *Century*'s editors, the depression signaled something more basic than a temporary malfunctioning of the capitalist system; it was indicative of fundamental flaws in the system itself. For that system, based on acquisitiveness and unrestrained competition, inevitably resulted in an unfair distribution of wealth. And although the market crash was more a symptom than a cause of the crisis, the church had been complicit in the speculative frenzy that precipitated the crash: "The people who were gambling most recklessly sat in its pews, and never felt the slightest incongruity between their presence at worship on Sunday and their luck in the profit-chase during the rest of the week" (November 25, 1931).

As a remedy for "the breakdown of our competitive order," the *Century*, in a March 11, 1931, editorial, came out strongly in favor of a managed national economy:

> It is time to cry aloud for an end to the era of laissez faire and the unhindered individualism of profit-seeking production. It is time for the preaching of a new evangelism—the evangelism of the voluntary liquidation of the competitive system in order that there may be a planned economy which shall insure to every person in the nation an adequate supply of the goods of life.

Although few specifics were given for such an economic plan—and no suggestions on how to bring about the "voluntary liquidation" of the old system—the magazine was clearly championing a socialist ideal. In the same issue theologian John Bennett gave reasons why Christianity and socialism need each other. And the very next week an editorial titled "Two Years of Mr. Hoover," while finding the president to be a man of conscience and courage, nonetheless took him to task for his "almost naïve confidence" in private and competitive enterprise and his "morbid fear of socialism."

I T MIGHT SEEM surprising, then, that editor Charles Clayton Morrison endorsed Hoover for re-election in 1932. But Morrison believed that despite the Republican incumbent's adherence to "rugged individualism" and his overly cautious approach to the depression, he would be more liberal—or at least more responsibly conservative—than Democrat Franklin D. Roosevelt. The editor feared that if elected, Roosevelt would go to the White House "under enormous obligations to the most sinister figure in American life—[newspaper publisher] William Randolph Hearst"; the Hearst "black shadow" would be cast over his entire foreign policy (October 5, 1932). Also, if Hoover had unfortunately retreated to an equivocal position on the prohibition issue, Roosevelt was all too unequivocal—on the wrong (i.e., the wet) side. (Repeal of prohibition came about in 1933, but it was no doubt inevitable, regardless of who was elected in '32. Nonenforcement, bootlegging and disdain had taken their toll, turning a Protestant triumph into a major defeat and shaking Protestant self-confidence. With hindsight, the *Century* editorialized that the Eighteenth Amendment was an inadequate, unwise and undemocratic method of effecting federal control of the liquor traffic; but this was a noticeable change of tune, for the magazine had long supported the amendment.)

Again in '32 Norman Thomas was the Socialist candidate. Morrison much admired Thomas and shared most of his views, but he regarded the two-party system as essential to American government, corrupt and self-seeking though that system might be. No third party could be effective, he felt, unless it displaced one of the major parties—in which case it would become a competitor for power, with its idealism and sincerity certain to be "diluted with opportunism and corrupted with the lust of office and the greed for the spoils of office" (October 19, 1932). Managing editor Hutchinson, who in 1932 joined the socialist Chicago-Call-to-Action Movement, did back Thomas that year—a fact that was not acknowledged in the *Century,* however, until *after* the fact, in a casual reference in a book review (October 3, 1934).

In a series of editorials beginning in the spring of '32, the *Century* envisioned and promoted a different kind of third party—a party without candidates, a party representing disinterested political principles rather than special interests. Intended to influence the two-party system constructively, the Disinterested Party would serve "as the organized and effective agency of progressive policies conceived and projected only for the well-being of the whole body politic," and it would be "protected against decadence by its renunciation of officeholding and patronage."

> The presence in our body politic of such a party is the only means by which democracy can be saved from its present moral chaos, from the tyranny of entrenched interests, from the insolence of a predatory officeholding party system, and from the peril of a fascist dictatorship of big business, on the one hand, or of a communist dictatorship of the proletariat, on the other [December 31, 1932].

The Disinterested Party would exist only for its platform, and it would endorse only those major-party candidates who accepted that platform. It would be a changing platform, responsive to the changing conditions of the nation and the world. The platform planks for '32 embodied a number of *Century* concerns: U.S. adherence to the World Court protocol; U.S. entry into the League of Nations, provided that its covenant be amended to eliminate military sanctions; U.S. recognition of the Soviet Union (which was granted a year later); the safeguarding of the rights of conscientious objectors (including those denied citizenship, such as Canadian-born theologian D. C. Macintosh of Yale Divinity School); the abolition of compulsory military training in state-supported educational institutions other than military and naval academies; emergency measures for relief and public-works employment; the securing of constitutional rights for minorities; the reduction of gross inequality of income by steeply progressive rates of taxation on large incomes; "progressive socialization of the ownership and control of natural resources, public utilities and basic industries"; "the nationalization of our entire banking system"; and so on (June 8, 1932).

During the thirties, theologian Reinhold Niebuhr, though himself a *Century* contributing editor at the time, became more

Reinhold Niebuhr (1892–1971)
RELIGIOUS NEWS SERVICE PHOTO

and more critical of the kind of social-gospel liberalism that
the journal had championed for decades. With his brand of
neo-orthodoxy Niebuhr was endeavoring to transform and re-
shape the social gospel rather than dispense with it entirely,
but he deplored what he saw as its shallow optimism, its naïve
idealism, its moral absolutism. His objection to the proposal
for a Disinterested Party foreshadowed more intense debates

49

that were to come. From the standpoint of political realism, said Niebuhr, the proposal is "pure moonshine."

> It represents the inevitable confusion of middle-class intellectualism which imagines that political changes are achieved by the united efforts of good people who bring pressure to bear upon traditional political parties. Such a hope completely ignores the economic basis of politics and the political inefficacy of nonpartisan action [November 9, 1932].

A lengthy editorial comment appended to Niebuhr's criticism contended that the *Century* shared his presupposition about the economic basis of politics and that in several ways he had misconceived the magazine's thesis concerning the Disinterested Party. In any case, nothing like that party was ever launched on a truly national scale, although something resembling its *modus vivendi* may be seen today in various states in independent-voter organizations.

Put on the defensive by Niebuhr's assaults on liberalism, the *Century* sought to counter him in various ways. For example, it argued that liberalism, contrary to its critics, is not a system of doctrines but simply a method of inquiry—a free method unbound by orthodoxy's rigid and authoritarian norms. Moreover, it maintained, Niebuhr himself relied on that method; he surely had not arrived at his views via fundamentalism. The magazine was right in saying that Niebuhr was essentially a liberal, but it was wrong in reducing theological liberalism to a method, for liberalism manifestly had doctrines and presuppositions of its own.

ROOSEVELT'S MARGIN of victory in 1932 was so large that he was not beholden to William Randolph Hearst or anyone else. Relieved that their fears had been unwarranted, the *Century*'s editors became more and more enthusiastic about the new president and his New Deal policies. This support was not uncritical, however. Perceiving the president to be a trial-and-error experimenter more inclined to tinker with capitalism than to replace it, the magazine voiced concern that he might not move far enough toward socialism. Singling out capitalism as "the reason of our misery," it hoped that Roosevelt would have the courage to carry out a government takeover of business should that prove necessary.

The *Century* interpreted the results of the off-year elections of 1934 as giving Roosevelt a clear-cut mandate that said, "Go left, Mr. President, go left"; it asserted that "many features of the 1934 election suggest that a union of forces for a vigorous offensive in support of an avowedly radical program is not impossible" (November 14, 1934). Of the "alphabet soup" of federal agencies initiated by Roosevelt, not all found equal favor with the publication; it was, for instance, doubtful about the National Recovery Administration long before the Supreme Court pronounced that agency's death sentence (even so, it carried the NRA eagle sign on its second page for many months). But the *Century* lauded the government's taking a direct role in the development of natural resources in such innovative projects as the Tennessee Valley Authority. Concluded managing editor Hutchinson in a three-part series on the TVA: "The projectors of this many-sided venture have a real chance to produce, on a scale to command imitation, a new order of life for this country" (April 25, 1934).

How was this "new order of life," this new economic system, to come about? According to the *Century,* "the new system calls pre-eminently for an economic man of cooperative, unselfish self-restraint, operating in a limited market determined according to a social plan," and the only agency in the United States capable of calling forth that individual was the Christian church: "The function of the Christian church is to provide the new economic man whose birth and growth will match the birth and growth of the new economic system." This, the magazine affirmed, "is the moment for which the social gospel has been waiting" (October 11, 1933). Furthermore: "If the Christian church once sees what is involved, it will find here the most challenging moral issue with which it has ever come to grips, the issue of persuading its members to the actual renunciation of profits, voluntarily, on behalf of the general good" (August 30, 1933). The paper was also of the opinion that "the step from the Roosevelt system to a true and candid socialization of the economic system would be a much easier one to take than is generally realized" (January 17, 1934).

Critics on the *Century*'s left differed with the magazine on how to reach the goals they shared with it; its notion of

51

"revolution" was for them too evolutionary and too painless. The New Deal did not, in their estimate, constitute the hardest step in bringing about a socialized economic system; the idealistic weekly was sidestepping the crucial issues of class conflict and the factor of coercion in effecting social justice. And they were highly skeptical about the possibility of persuading middle-class Protestants—most of whom were to the right of Roosevelt—to forego profits voluntarily.

By 1937, however, labor had made such gains, "corporation buccaneering" had been so greatly curbed, and the administration had so radically reformed American capitalism that the *Century* was no longer calling for even an evolutionary revolution; it was already under way.

Once it became clear that the new capitalism would not be left entirely in the hands of capitalists, editor Morrison seemed able to live with it. The *Century* was less politically ideological in 1937 than it had been in 1933 and 1934. But if it largely accommodated itself to Roosevelt's domestic programs and policies, it was often uneasy with his foreign policy (except for his "good neighbor" policy toward Latin America, which it heartily approved of). Even in endorsing him for re-election in 1936, the magazine expressed "profound disquiet" over his "big-navy proclivities." Noting that "all along the international horizon flashes the lightning of coming storm," the editors worried about the weaknesses of the nation's neutrality legislation and wondered whether its farmers and industrialists would be able to resist the moneymaking opportunities of a wartime situation (November 11, 1936). As domestic policy and foreign policy seemed to merge in an armaments policy designed as a "quick fix" to restore prosperity and end unemployment, the peace-oriented journal found the cure worse than the malady. Apprehensive from the time of Roosevelt's "portentous" talk in Chicago in October 1937 about quarantining Japan—and fearful of a "repetition of the folly of 1917"—it broke with the president, eventually terming him the Führer of an inchoate fascism.

CALAMITOUS though the depression was for the U.S., the *Century*'s editors gave no less attention during the thirties to major happenings abroad—and most of those were calamitous, too. The depression itself had disastrous consequences elsewhere, especially in Europe, and in Germany the economic predicament and the resulting social malaise contributed to the rise of Adolf Hitler and the Third Reich. Events such as Japan's occupation of Manchuria in 1931 and its gradual penetration of China proper, coupled with Italy's mid-decade conquest of Ethiopia, demonstrated the virtual uselessness of the Kellogg-Briand Pact of 1928, even though almost all of the world's nations—including Japan and Italy—had ratified it, thereby proclaiming their renunciation of war. Having labored long and hard to promote and publicize the peace pact, the *Century* was hard put to acknowledge its ineffectiveness. Nonetheless it did so, saying that the pact was part of a peace structure based on the unsound presupposition that the plighted word of nations may be trusted, and that it had lost prestige since it was negotiated (October 16 and November 6, 1935).

During this period the *Century* followed closely the progress of Mahatma Gandhi's effort to gain India's independence from Britain; though that effort had its ups and downs, it was one development on the international scene that the journal could be positive about. Primarily because of his espousal of nonviolent resistance, the Mahatma became a model of religious heroism for the *Century* and many of its readers. When he caused a split in his movement by putting the independence struggle "on hold" in order to crusade in behalf of his country's "untouchable" castes, the paper lavished praise on him:

> He has once more challenged the spiritual stupor of mankind. He did it before with his claim that the achievement of vast national purposes is not dependent upon resort to force. Here he penetrates to an even more greatly needed spiritual principle, namely, that the doing of justice must precede the gaining of justice. He stands in the direct succession of that prophet who saw that judgment must begin in the house of God, and of the even greater prophet who saw that blessing at the altar requires a prior establishment of right relations with the socially wronged [October 3, 1934].

The editors found Gandhi to be an embodiment of the Sermon on the Mount, but frequent contributor John Haynes Holmes went even further and touted him as "the Christ of modern times" (November 25, 1931). Understandably, this was too much for some readers, who sent in letters objecting to Holmes's deification of the Indian leader, however noble and saintly he might be.

Initially, *Century* editors, like many other observers, underestimated the Nazi menace. In 1932, when Hitler was offered the chancellorship of Germany but seemed unlikely to be able to form a Reichstag majority, the magazine maintained that the Nazis no longer threatened to function "as a genuinely fascist party" (November 30, 1932). The next year, when Hitler did accede to the chancellorship, it editorialized that the necessary compromises of parliamentary politics had already taken the terror out of him (February 8, 1933). It saw him as no more than "a demagogue and a great political orator"— hardly a man equipped to give Germany "that strong leadership it wants so badly." Moreover: "The real German revolution is yet to come. . . . The third reich will certainly come, but Hitler is not likely to go down in history as its founder" (March 15, 1933).

Shortly, however, the extent of Hitler's triumph, and the gravity of the situation thus brought about, was all too clear. It was a triumph, said the *Century,* that the allies had brought on themselves—by refusing to take "the road of conciliation" and by making of the Versailles Treaty "nothing but a victors' vengeance," a "brutal betrayal" of the German people's confidence. "We who defeated Germany helped to make Hitler" (May 10, 1933). The journal denounced the Nazi regime's "unspeakable brutalities" against Jews, urged the U.S. government to provide haven for refugees and deportees, and called for a boycott of the 1936 Olympic Games in Germany. It kept tabs on the worsening circumstances of Germany's Protestant churches, and it commended the 6,000 pastors who dared to speak out against Hitler's creation of a state-controlled "German Church." At the same time it rebuked the pastors for opposing not Nazi totalitarianism *in toto* but only its encroachments on organized religion; they were making a truly heroic stand, but "the cause which they champion is not the fully Christian ideal" (February 7, 1934).

By 1935 the *Century* was excoriating Hitler in unequivocal terms: "The madman of Berlin has cast away the last shred of pacific pretense and has thrown down the gauntlet to

Europe." But though German rearmament, along with the increased military budgets of the allied powers, made war an "acute possibility," it was not inevitable: "The nations of Europe are all armed to the teeth, and still they cannot compel Germany to observe the terms of an unfair treaty. Something more is needed than weapons and more weapons, soldiers and more soldiers. Honest and equal disarmament has not been proved futile, for it has not been tried" (March 27, 1935). For the *Century* of Charles Clayton Morrison, war was never inevitable until the shooting began. "War, even in these dangerous days, is still as unnecessary as it is wicked" (April 8, 1936).

An appeal published in the October 7, 1931, Century

Hundreds Have Signed This; Will You?

To the President and Congress of the United States:

The recent decision of the Supreme Court, which denies the right of citizenship to persons who refuse to abdicate their conscience on the question of participation in armed conflict, forces us, the undersigned citizens, to notify the constituted authorities of our nation that we share the convictions of those who have been denied citizenship.

Some of the undersigned find it impossible, because of religious and moral scruples, to render any kind of combatant service in time of war. Others share the conviction of one of the persons denied citizenship in the recent Supreme Court decision and cannot promise support to the government until they have had the opportunity of weighing the moral issues involved in an international struggle.

We concur in the minority opinion of the Supreme Court that "in the forum of conscience, duty to a moral power higher than the state has always been maintained. The reservation of that supreme obligation, as a matter of principle, would undoubtedly be made by many of our conscientious citizens. The essence of religion is belief in a relation to God involving duties superior to those arising from any human relation."

. . . .

Finding myself in agreement with the foregoing statement concerning a decision of the Supreme Court with regard to conscientious objectors to war, I desire to have my name added as a signatory.

Name. . . . .

Position. . . . .

Street Address. . . . .

City and State. . . . .

But when the hoped-for disarmament did not material-
ize—and as Europe seemed to rush toward the precipice—the
magazine took refuge in neutralist sentiment. During the Span-
ish Civil War of 1936–39—a war that was a kind of dress
rehearsal for World War II—it declared that its sympathies
were "wholeheatedly" with the duly elected republican government; it detested "this Franco revolt," which was going
forward in large part because of aid from fascist Germany and
Italy. Nonetheless, "it is the duty of the United States to maintain a zone of sanity in a world going mad by keeping out of
war of any description in any place" (January 27, 1937). Ultimately—and ironically, given the publication's longtime in-
ternationalist stance—that neutralism was hard to distinguish
from isolationism. It held to that position until the attack on
Pearl Harbor.

R ECOILING REMORSEFULLY from the churches' all-
out support of militarism and nationalism in World War I,
many mainstream Protestants committed themselves, in vary-
ing degrees, to Christian pacifism in the twenties and thirties.
Denominational assemblies decried war as contrary to the will
of God and the mind of Christ; thousands of pastors and students signed pledges vowing never to take up arms; the interdenominational pacifist organization known as the Fellowship
of Reconciliation flourished. Reinhold Niebuhr, more and more
convinced that the law of love cannot be an absolute guide of
conduct in social morality and politics, defected from the
ranks of the FOR early in 1934 and became a kind of *bête
noire* to pacifists—especially to those who claimed that pacifism was politically adequate. That same year, however, Niebuhr was also at pains to differentiate his neo-orthodox thinking
from that of Karl Barth. Although Barth himself was one of
Hitlerism's "most determined foes," Barthian theology abetted
Hitler's type of reactionary politics: "Here," said Niebuhr,
"religious absolutism which begins by making the conscience
sensitive to all human weakness ends in complacency toward
social injustice" (June 6, 1934).

The *Century* absorbed a Christian socialist periodical,
the *World Tomorrow,* in August of that year, and its editor in
chief, Kirby Page, a noted pacifist, became a *Century* con-

tributing editor. Niebuhr and Page had been colleagues on the *World Tomorrow*; now both were on the *Century*'s masthead, presenting sharply contrasting points of view in the magazine. But partly as a result of the Niebuhrian onslaught, Page, though staunchly adhering to pacifism, gradually relinquished the claim to political relevance; for the Christian, pacifism was the way of the cross, the way of discipleship. The rationale was not peace at any price, but love at all costs.

Editor Morrison's own position differed from that of both Niebuhr and Page, though it was closer to Page's. He shared the pacifists' convictions about the sinfulness of war, but he did not eschew the use of force in all circumstances and he never joined the FOR, despite numerous invitations and entreaties; he thought of himself as a pragmatic noninterventionist rather than as an absolute pacifist. His peace stand stemmed from his conception of the church, and to him the church was a distinctive amalgam of religion and culture, best exemplified in America. His primary concern was to prevent the church from becoming captive to secular forces, to preserve its freedom of action as an instrument of the social gospel—and "the most acute aspect of the church's subservient relation to the political state . . . is that of war." Widespread renunciation of war would go far toward persuading both church and society of the fact that "the Christian allegiance is to a sovereignty which transcends all other sovereignties" (May 30, 1934). Going to war, Morrison felt, would mean the destruction of democracy and morality at home; America would no longer be true to itself, would no longer be the Promised Land: "We have discovered that our goodness, our moralism, is in large measure the expression of our relative detachment. . . . We are no more virtuous than others. The difference is a difference in circumstances" (October 20, 1937). Different circumstances? To Niebuhr, that claim suggested a special blessing, a special grace, for America, and it smacked of self-righteousness.

The decade of the thirties saw the gradual disintegration of the social-gospel synthesis. At first the traumas of the depression afforded a rallying cry for church liberals, but divisions soon developed over the question of class struggle and the use of coercion—divisions that were to deepen as the world situation darkened and war loomed on the horizon. "Crisis theology," or neo-orthodoxy, was making inroads even in the pages of *The Christian Century*, and by decade's end Morrison himself was calling for a "new liberalism," for the old had become static and sterile—an instance of arrested development. In any case, to his credit, he continued to open the *Century*'s pages to a wide variety of viewpoints—even the views of those who, like Reinhold Niebuhr, often looked upon the magazine's editorial opinions and proposals as "pure moonshine." ∎

War's Dilemmas:
The *Century* 1938-1945

MARTIN E. MARTY

O NE COULD DRAW a figurative line through the topics
covered in most weekly issues of *The Christian Century*
from the year before World War II through the end of that war.
On one side would be all evidences of the war: conscientious
chronicling of its main events—especially where religion had
a bearing—coupled with articles and editorials on issues of
war and peace. On the other side of this line would be hundreds
of reports on Christian church life and American culture. While
the latter have no "business as usual" stamp, since the war
colored almost everything those years, one senses that the
editors were saying: life must go on; faith needs nurture; the
subtleties of life matter; there are trenches in America as well
as on the front lines.

Between the wars a broad pacifist sentiment had developed. Protestant clergy, often coached or rallied by this most
influential mainline and liberal magazine, leaned toward the
peacemaking side. By the end of the 1930s, however, it was
a set of troubled peace people who commented here each
week.

The magazine's most noted off-premises editor, Reinhold
Niebuhr, was restless and, in the end, emphatic. For him pac-

Dr. Marty is a Century *senior editor and professor of the history
of Christianity at the University of Chicago Divinity School.*

ifism did not answer Hitler's demonic threat and the totalitarian evils. Few incidents in the magazine's history attracted as much attention as the break between editor Charles Clayton Morrison and Niebuhr. For several years Niebuhr's disaffection was evident, as he transferred loyalties to secular liberal magazines like the *Nation*. Then in 1941 he helped found and became editor of *Christianity and Crisis*.

The *Century* editors had the harder time of it, because they fully shared the Niebuhrians' horror of Nazism, fascism and Japanese militarism. And, throughout the 1930s, something in their editorial bones kept telling them that the issues would not be settled nor Hitler's aggression stopped without resistance. Many an editorial therefore warned, mourned or rued, but never offered useful alternatives to the war party's policies. If there was a consistent line, it was a progressive acquiescence to the inevitable, as Austria, Czechoslovakia, then Poland and so much of the rest of Europe fell. Let there be restraint, and a minimum of righteous fervor and self-idolatry as this "tragic necessity" unfolds, was the plea.

Part of the long-range philosophical outlook of Morrison and company was revealed when, once war came, they almost immediately began talking about its aftermath. While they could do little except to call for repentant participation and conscientious attention to the military prosecution of the war, the editors believed the Christian community had a great responsibility for subsequent peacemaking. Articles on how to wage peace, promote relief and structure international dialogue were frequent.

I T IS REVEALING to see how alert the magazine was to events in the Pacific theater. Forty-five years later, with so many mainstream Protestants apathetic or uncertain about the meaning of "foreign missions," it is hard to re-create a climate in which missionary thought played such a vivid role. Protestantism had a heavy investment in Japan, a commanding and literate nation that would be crucial for any Christian future in that hemisphere.

The editors long feared the Japanese military growth, and criticized American arms policies that curiously contributed to that buildup, even as President Franklin D. Roosevelt was scored for undue belligerence against Japan. There were notices that explained Shinto, the religious ethos and structure that supported Japanese nationalism and militarism. The fate of the Japanese churches, which were increasingly less autonomous, was a regular topic. Meanwhile, editors watched the situation of the church in China, long a favored missionary field. Reports indicated anti-Christian action by the Chinese communists, and many writers speculated whether much of the faith would survive the war, no matter its outcomes.

At the same time, specific aspects of the European—especially the German—war machines led editors to focus on them. Germany, Italy and, in its own way, Russia were totalitarianisms born in millennium-old Christian cultures. The editors considered it imperative to discern what went wrong after 1914 to bring into power Mussolini, Hitler and Stalin with all their instruments of terror.

The November 30, 1938, issue clearly spelled out in great detail the editors' thoughts on "Demonic Germany and the Predicament of Humanity":

> That such a phenomenon as the anti-Semitic pogrom could appear in Western society seemed at first incredible—in a society that has been for centuries impregnated with the principles of the Christian faith.

It was the announced intention to do away with Judaism and Jews that elicited the adjective "demonic" and charges of "hellishness." The editors strained their vocabularies to find language that—while none could capture the atrocity of Nazism—at least could serve as barometers and thermometers.

L IKE MOST other thoughtful Americans—Christian, Jewish, secular, public or private—the editors talked themselves into bemusement about how to respond. The "fiendish and shameless relapse from the most elemental instincts which actuate civilized humanity," when voiced by Josef Goebbels, left the West without a policy. Goebbels would export the Jews en masse to any takers. What to do? A few called for a preemptive attack on Germany. The editors were too pacific to encourage that and too practical to anticipate success at whatever price. The Western powers had "everything to lose in defeat and nothing to gain in victory."

A vandalized synagogue in Munich in the thirties
ARCHIVES, CITY OF MUNICH

The editors looked at proposals for a Jewish homeland in Madagascar, some spot in South Africa, Tanganyika or Australia, but saw few prospects. "Palestine is out of the question, in view of the failure of the British mandate to attain some *modus vivendi* as between Jews and Arabs." The United States, they thought, should take more exiles, but with ten million already unemployed, the arrival of hundreds of thousands of Jewish exiles would only exacerbate that problem and stimulate anti-Semitism. So they offered little direction: "We make no attempt to disguise our bafflement."

This early editorial stance on a Jewish homeland confronts one of the touchiest issues left over from those years. The editors could say "Palestine is out of the question," then spend many issues debating whether it really was, and ways in which it was *in* the question. They have been much attacked for their attitudes during this period; my shelf has several books criticizing Americans, Christians, liberals and *The Christian Century* for being blind, or for having knowledge but no policy concerning the Jews.

One hesitates to minimize the burden of moral failure in the Christian and Protestant past. At the same time, encountering freshly the thousands of pages from, as it were, the other direction temporally, sets the issue in context.

The *Century* editors were agents of interfaith amity and victims of an obsolete model. They thought they were tolerant, and were, on any reading of the Jewish-Christian temperatures of the 1930s. They tirelessly supported interfaith organizations, unwearyingly opposed domestic anti-Semitism, and were hopeful about concord and respect in the country's future. On the other hand, they were captive of turn-of-the-century WASP models that called for assimilation, accommodation, homogeneity in American life.

From the beginning, such Protestants were very friendly to Jews, but only Jews of a particular sort. Theirs was the Reform Jewish world, which, it must be remembered, was dominated by passionate anti-Zionists right into the beginning of this period. For them, Judaism was a universal faith, not given to ethnic particularism and thickness. In a way, Judaism could draw on its heritage to be as much like liberal Protestantism as possible, while liberal Protestantism drew on its heritage to be more like Reform Judaism than one imagines could have been possible in that intolerant age.

Such an outlook meant that the editors thought they were being friendly to all Jews but Zionists. The magazine regularly published articles like Morris S. Lazaron's contribution to the famed "How My Mind Has Changed in This Decade" series on August 30, 1939. Judaism, wrote the rabbi, was a universal religion. Jewish nationalism was a reaction to despair, but it could not preserve Judaism. "Judaism cannot accept as the instrument of its salvation the very philosophy of nationalism which is leading the world to destruction. Shall we condemn it as Italian or German but accept it as Jewish?" With the editors he praised the Zionists' marvels in Palestine but warned World Zionist Organization extremists of perils that lay ahead.

Judaism was "not an exclusive, nationalist . . . tribal faith," and the Zionist solution threatened to change this.

Given this background, it would have been bizarre and intellectually fickle for the editors to reverse their position instantly on the homeland question. "For Judaism to insist rigorously on aloofness, on segregation, on maintaining itself as a self-enclosed community, is to withhold its witness from the general community," proclaimed an editorial of December 20, 1939.

I N A CELEBRATED incident, the editors had difficulty believing Holocaust statistics presented by a rare Reform Zionist, Stephen Wise. The editors checked with the state department and accepted the department's verdict that Wise was probably exaggerating. That aside, there was little minimizing. In 1938 the editors began constant reports on the little evidence available about pogroms and eventual threats of extermination of Jews. They simply could see no "just and moral solution" of the Jewish homeland issue. The problem, they said, resulted from deceitful policies that made Jews the tragic pawns of empire (May 31, 1939).

In "Gazing into the Pit" (May 9, 1945), the editor found visual corroboration of what he had feared about and reported on concentration camps.

> What can be said that will not seem like tossing little words up against a giant mountain of ineradicable evil? . . . We have found it hard to believe that the reports . . . could be true. Almost desperately we have tried to think that they must be wildly exaggerated.

The editors had feared atrocity-mongering of the World War I sort. "But such puny barricades cannot stand up against the terrible facts." They called for every kind of Christian ecumenical response. The magazine's approach through the Holocaust years was limited, blinded, and the editors were benumbed. So was the U.S. government; more so were other Christian periodicals that almost or entirely ignored the subject. Even Jewish organizations knew little to do, and most did little. Liberal Protestants had their limits and villainies, but singling them out, out of context, for condemnation does not do justice to the larger story.

On the domestic scene—and on an infinitely smaller and less ominous scale—the magazine kept up its non-shooting war with the other large group of Americans who created problems for assimilators and seekers of homogeneity: Catholics. Liberal Protestantism and *The Christian Century* have a partly earned reputation for unreasoned anti-Catholicism, and the war years show that there was not a total cease-fire on this front.

Certainly one myth characterized their approach and limited their ecumenical and civil outreach. Like most non-Catholics, they thought that the Roman Catholic church, and especially its American branch, was a monolith, a juggernaut, a subservient mass. Culturally and socially, the editors thought, Catholics should be nondescript, blended and tolerant—like liberal Protestants. The reality of Catholic life, in other words, was very different from the image it bore.

That said, except for one incident and its frantic response, the magazine was far more genial and friendly to Catholicism than its reputation indicates. While it would not have occurred to the editors to include Catholics in church unity schemes and pictures, they showed respect for Popes Pius XI and XII, wished Catholic citizens well, and often praised the church's achievements. What ruined everything for a year was the proposal by Franklin Roosevelt to appoint Myron C. Taylor as a Vatican ambassador. In 1940 the entire possibility looked like breaking the game rules of national life. The magazine returned to this theme so frequently that on this one subject alone this reader of fifteen year's worth of issues announces: it was a bore. No harm done, one might say, except to imagination and variety.

The editors were not solely interested in confirmation that the monolithic juggernaut, under signals from Rome, always acted against the American Protestant Republic. Just the opposite. The Morrison era found the staff eager to report on ferment and change. It is impressive to see how early they began watching the late Father John Courtney Murray, S.J. On January 5, 1944, the magazine reported on a pamphlet in which Murray and a colleague showed how Catholics would collaborate with all who believe in God in order to "renovate secular society." Protestants ought to go along with this pro-

John Courtney Murray, S. J. (1904–1967)
COURTESY WOODSTOCK COLLEGE

gram, the magazine advised, even if they should remain cautious.

On August 1, 1945, a long editorial gave thoughtful praise to Murray's pamphlet "Freedom of Religion." Murray's essay was "so keen in analysis, so fine in spirit and so clear in expression that it not only exhibits the issues without evasion or distortion but also helps to create an atmosphere in which these issues can be discussed dispassionately." This did not mean that Murray converted the editors to the half-way house he portrayed; he himself was not pushing as hard as he did successfully twenty years later when Vatican II essentially approved his approach. Differences remained. Yet there was a fine discrimination growing in the editors' minds.

T HIS REFERENCE to Catholicism is the first turn to the other half of the magazine's concerns. While monitoring the war and its devastations, the *Century* stayed faithful to the day-to-day doings of Americans in culture and church. While the domestic issues that concerned the editors had continuity with those of prewar years, they were necessarily de-emphasized during the crisis. The magazine cajoled believers into feeding more of the hungry, drying up the wet (liquor interests regularly were scored), and there were editorals about lynchings and labor, gambling and injustice. To their credit, the writers kept alert on the fronts where demagogues like Charles Coughlin still found followings, and blasted his anti-Semitism and divisive social policies. The shadow of late depression days remained, though by 1938 there seemed to be little new to say.

One of my favorite and one of the most revealing stories in the *Century's* lore occurred when Charles Clayton Morrison looked back on thirty years of editing (October 5, 1938):

> I recall with many an inward chuckle, one morning some ten or a dozen years ago when the business manager came into the office to tell of a dream he had had that night. It seems that I was drowning in Lake Michigan. He and my editorial colleagues were standing on the shore, having exhausted all their efforts to rescue me. I was just going down for the third and last time, but before the water covered my mouth I thrust up my hand and cried, "Keep it religious! Keep it religious!"
>
> They knew that "it" meant *The Christian Century*, and that my exhortation was in keeping with the determination, shared by us all, against the temptation to break away from religious journalism and make the paper an organ of secular idealism. I speak of it as a "temptation," for that it truly was. Our public could easily have been expanded far beyond the church, our income greatly increased, and our secular prestige enhanced, had the collective abilities represented in our editorial staff been devoted to a free-lance type of journalism.

Maybe. In any case, the good doctor added, "We have been able to resist this temptation because our hearts are in the Christian church," whose problems and hopes the magazine chose to share and stick with.

Sometimes this emphasis meant celebrating the occasional moments of victory on the front the magazine held most dear: the ecumenical. Very little ecumenical news missed mention. In 1939 this could mean something as in-house as the reunion of northern and southern Methodists. Yet never did the editors feel compelled to give Federal Council of Churches officials or planners for the World Council of Churches a free ride; criticism was constant. One could reduce the length of reporting on this subject, which took hundreds of pages, by saying that if unity in Christ was being approached or offered, this magazine was for it. The mark of "one" sometimes obscured "holy," "catholic," or "apostolic" in the editors' concerns.

No surprises there. There were surprises, though, in the way these chastened liberals talked about the mission of the church. Far from being the naturalist theists their teachers may have been, Morrison, Winfred Ernest Garrison, Paul Hutchinson and new young writers, like Harold E. Fey, were devoted more to what Henry Pitney Van Dusen elsewhere described as Christocentric liberalism. They were particularists who seemed to think that this could be the core of a universal message, and they stuck to it.

WHOEVER HAS laughed at a philosophy of history betrayed in the name *Christian Century* or at the simple-mindedness of modernism would do well to read the editors struggling with theological change around and in them. The critical realism of the Niebuhr brothers, the neo-orthodoxy of Karl Barth and the Europeans, the recovery of Søren Kierkegaard—each of whom was closely watched by *Century* book reviewers—must have been difficult for these midwestern Disciples and Methodists to grasp. Comfortable with immanental views of God, they struggled with "Wholly Other" kinds of transcendence. Nurtured toward sunny faith in human disposition, under God, they confronted the revived emphasis on original sin, total depravity and the human condition as diminishing the grandeur of the human as God's creation.

The famous, and almost eternal, "How My Mind Has Changed" series patented in the late 1930s could have made the editors look like mere tenders of a theological cafeteria line. But Morrison and his co-workers did more than print articles; they argued with the authors, plundering, ransacking, resisting—and sometimes being changed themselves.

In other areas, too, the *Century* was open to change. For example, it maintained a respectable record of placing women on the editorial staff; when Margaret Frakes was hired in 1949 she was the publication's fourth female editor. This was during a time when there were practically no female professors at U.S. seminaries. Not until August 23, 1939, had the editors been able to cheer Georgia Harkness's appointment at Garrett Biblical Institute in Evanston as that of the first woman on an American seminary staff. And then they readily printed a letter saying that no, Professor Harkness was not the first. What about Margaret Tappan, who had been at San Francisco Theological Seminary since 1937? Editorials like "Women in the Church" (December 11, 1940) furthered the cause; it carried the following indictment: "The American church is still one of the most backward of all institutions in the place it accords to women and the attitude which it exhibits toward them."

ONE UNANTICIPATED shift in these years brought public attention to evangelicalism, fundamentalism and Pentecostalism at the expense of the Protestant mainstream. The editors saw fundamentalism as a backwoods, over the hill, jerkwater phenomenon that had already outlived its time. There were several articles on "Holy Rollers" in the remote distance, and some of their churches were congratulated for serving overlooked people. However, C. P. Raycito urged that "we must not compromise with our convictions just because these primitive notions of the minor sects seem to be gaining in popularity or because they do attract some we cannot reach" (August 15, 1939). To surrender to the fundamentalists' otherworldly outlook would be as bad, the author thought, as succumbing to the fashionable defeatism of European theology. There was a mention that Carl McIntire was organizing

a fundamentalist American Council of Christian Churches, but
it seemed a curiosity. Harold E. Fey reported at length on
"Youth for Christ" in the June 20, 1945, issue and he managed
to say some good things about revivalism, but worried about
the slickness and crowd manipulation; it was "milky abstrac-
tion" compared to the solid meat of Jonathan Edwards, Francis
Asbury or even Dwight L. Moody. Fey made one bad guess:
"One is entitled to doubt that the current resurgence will en-
dure very long."

What impresses is the intactness of the mainstream Protestant world. With passion rarely amassed today, the editors
and those people important to them held huge rallies in downtown auditoriums. They evangelized and witnessed and pro-
grammed and cheered; they were the custodians of the culture's
spiritual values, and that task required unity. They worried
about keeping the Protestant colleges alive, finding postwar
ministers and representing religion on campuses, where minds
were being shaped. They watched every move in the seminaries and divinity schools, because leadership training mat-
tered greatly.

The Christian Century, through its good-natured Quintus
Quiz columns, thousands of book reviews and hundreds of
editorials, saw itself as a fine-tuner of these impulses. That
required the editors to be more self-critical than I, for one,
had been led to picture them as being. There was some or-
neriness, cantankerousness and sometimes willful self-blind-
ing in Morrison, whom a few of those who contribute to the
magazine, I among them, remember at least dimly. In his
nineties and almost blind, he could storm off the elevator,
attacking us "young fellows" who, he thought, were compli-
cating his world by advocating relations with Orthodox, evangelicals and Catholics. He loved an argument, spoiled for a
fight and took disagreements over values as seriously as he
would have taken training for the Olympics. All that was true,
and yet he had his supple side.

I N THAT SPIRIT the editors distanced themselves on February 2, 1938, from facile old modernisms that only wanted
to be tied to science and progress. "There is no more pathetic
spectacle than is afforded by those liberals of the old school

who still defend" this wan theism, they wrote. The editorial admired Martin Niemöller's Berlin congregation whose power to oppose Hitler came from the very act of worship with use of the creed, " 'I believe in God the Father Almighty, maker of heaven and earth.' (Its pastor is in jail for affirming this same creed.) No listless verbalism here! The ancient creed has become new!"

On those terms the magazine attacked John D. Rockefeller, Jr., for a New York speech in which he suggested that the church drop creeds, liturgies and devotion for the sake of "unselfish good works" (April 25, 1945). The editorial gave Rockefeller, after a few pats, a strong crash course on the role of belief and worship: "Christianity is not morality, not even the morality of Jesus—though it inspires morality." Nor is it philanthropy or social action. Rockefeller should have attacked sectarian misuse of creeds, not creeds per se. This is not faith in the teacher, but faith "which his death and his resurrection" created and evoked, and still does.

> This is the Christian gospel, and it is the primary and supreme mission of the church to bring all men into the orbit of its saving power, to declare it to the world until mankind accepts Jesus Christ as the cornerstone, not of the church alone, but of civilization itself.

Accuse the writers of imperialism in faith one might, but not of timidity.

A February 9 follow-up on "Evangelizing the Church" shows as well as anything that when Morrison said "keep it religious" he had a very distinct translation of "religious." He could be friendly to other faiths, but he could not picture a redeemed world apart from a faithful church. It was time to call the church back "from its wanderings in the wilderness of secular ideologies to its historic and essential character." Progressivism was out.

Almost never did the magazine refer to "religious revival," a constant theme after 1952. But once, during the war, the editors pondered foxhole religion and the fact that "every analyst of religious trends in wartime notes a quickening of interest in religion in the minds of many persons who have hitherto been indifferent to it." In this August 25, 1943, editorial they did not feel called upon to challenge the sincerity of such religion. One could meet God in dire circumstances. A religion that was no good in time of trouble was no good at any time. "But the trouble with such belated discoveries of God in desperate emergencies is that [the converts] discover so little."

The dramas of war and peace were the plot of these years of *The Christian Century*. The quieter dramas of the normal circumstances of life made their exactions and offerings week after week. The fidelity of the editors to that somewhat more mundane world strikes me as having been as much a fulfillment of their vocation as chronicling the events of the war. Yes, Dr. Morrison, the legacy you handed over sounds strong and clear to successors: "Keep it religious!" So it was, and so it would be. ∎

Peace and Pluralism:
The *Century* 1946-1952

MARTIN E. MARTY

HISTORIANS MUST learn and teach others to judge the past in the context of the possibilities open to those living within it. To expect sixteenth-century people to be at home, for example, with modern interfaith relations or feminism is unrealistic and anachronistic. However, grading is still possible, where it is advisable or necessary: some sixteenth-century people did horribly with the possibilities then open to them. For instance, Luther and most of the Renaissance humanists were failures, even villains, in respect to Jews.

Overusing the gift of hindsight can also lead to condescension. Whoever sees everyone and everything in the past as silly should realize that on such terms all of us now alive will look silly a century from now—or minutes from now.

Temptations to look at this magazine's past with condescension are there. Many of *The Christian Century* editors' hopes failed them; the cities they would build turned to ashes; their dreams for benign and civil Christian futures were thwarted not only by the malice of others, but because they were themselves naïve.

Without dropping critical guard as I turned any of the thousands of pages produced between 1946 and 1952, and finding much to criticize, just as often a different impression and emotion overtook me. Awe. Awe for the extent of the coverage, the ambition, the relative consistency, the suppleness, the coherence of a Christian philosophy that did not match—or want to match—the emerging world. There were, admittedly, some howlers, and I'll mention one or two. There was occasional moral blindness, too much hope for human causes, and on and on. Yet consider the alternative: the meanness and short-sightedness of many people who did not dream dreams like the editors.

At mid-century, on January 4, 1950, the staff under editor Paul Hutchinson (Charles Clayton Morrison had stepped down in 1947 after forty years as editor) celebrated a half-century of being *The Christian Century.* They confessed nostalgic fondness for their original (1884–1900) name, the *Christian Oracle.* It was more fun, they joked, to pose as an oracle than to misname a century. "Viewed in the perspective furnished by fifty years, that optimism is now a far-off and almost forgotten thing. . . . We do not see a Christian century, either now or in any century." Time to throw in the towel? Hardly. "Nevertheless, to the task undertaken fifty years ago of bringing this century, and all time and all the aspects of man's life, under the rule of Christ, this paper remains committed. Forward to the Christian century!" And they continued. And here we are.

Religious life in the United States was changing dramatically in these years, as the religious community changed from a world of mainstream and established Protestant hegemony and privilege to one that openly acknowledged pervasive pluralism. The *Christian Century* editors, as the most plausible and responsible unofficial voices of what is today called "mainline Protestantism," had the task of educating their readers and themselves to live creatively with this great shift.

The editors were sometimes dragged screaming into this new era. Witness the editorial of June 13, 1951, the last full-throated defense of the old: "Pluralism—National Menace." "The idea of a plural society is so new to Americans that many will not even understand the term." The editors offered only a negative portrayal of pluralism—one modeled after the Dutch *Verzuiling.* (They didn't use the word, happily for their readers.) *Verzuiling* meant a columned life—a republic with complete and separate institutions for, say, Protestants and Catholics and Jews. Fearing that Catholic schools would form a strong base for a subculture, and worried about the decline

Paul Hutchinson, longtime managing editor and editor of the Century

of the public schools as the junior wing of American public religion's informal church establishment, the editors reared up.

A NOSTALGIA similar in ways to that of today's religious New Right was evident in the magazine. In the good old days, the editors believed, Americans spoke "the same language" and had "the same cultural background," as well as many other important "sames." The editors still favored immigration quotas to limit the lumps of peoplehood that could not be blended into homogeneous America. For a long time

75

the system had been successfully digestive; it could cope with non-Protestants as impotent minorities. But now Catholicism was large and powerful, with leaders who would "like to alter certain of the basic concepts upon which American democracy is founded." This was not quite the old nativism; the editors had no heart for that. Yet they could not swallow the changes easily.

Borrowing definitions from J. S. Furnivall, the editors thought pluralism was comprised of "two or more elements which live side by side, yet without mingling, in one political unit." Such a society can have "no common will"; anomie and instability will result, with union only on fiscal concerns or national defense. How then express a social will? How be other than vulnerable to communist or other ideological propaganda? Blaming Catholics for proliferation of Catholic parochial schools, labor unions, civic clubs, veterans' organizations and political lobbies, the editors feared that Protestants would compensate with their own self-interest groups. The editors did not notice the extent to which these already existed, and that, in a way, they were speaking for what no longer was the "same" America, but one particular set of interests. Yet through all these years in subtler editorials and choice of articles, they showed awareness of that changing world.

On some fronts, there were many things to cheer. Scores of pages were devoted to the organizations that at mid-century advocated a republic in which all humans had hope. Similarly, for people like *Christian Century* writers and readers, there were reasons to hope that much human harmonizing would unite behind symbols associated specifically with the Christian church and the name of Christ. Polite, mannered and tolerant about most world religions (if nervous about a more aggressive Islam), the magazine betrayed a kind of Christian triumphal or imperial bearing. No other religion could do as much as Christianity to promote justice and peace. Then, the editors could turn around and criticize Christianity—including their own kind—for its apathy and moral flaws.

Today the concept of a federation seems farfetched. Invoking visions of "spaceship earth" or "global village" or *United* Nations or *World* Council of Churches or the *oikoumene* of ecumenism sets oneself up to be marked as naïve, silly or utopian. At mid-century, however, there were signs that people might begin transcending denominational, tribal and national boundaries for common survival and interests.

And the naïve, silly and utopian *Christian Century* editors cheered. With almost wearying frequency they monitored, criticized, reported on and hoped for the United Nations, UNESCO, and other "united" and "federated" agencies of state and church. The Korean War was another tragic setback for their hopes, but they were untiring.

Briefed to suspect them of unsophisticated leftism in world affairs, a reader will quickly find that the editors were suspicious of Marxism, had moved far from socialism—though they allowed some contributors to defend it—and were extremely critical of the Soviet Union. These were Senator Joseph McCarthy's prime years, and the editors stood guard against his encroachments on liberties. They hoped for progress after China's Communist Revolution, but always worried for liberties and for the Christian future there. If during the 1930s they had occasionally published articles that saw positive possibilities in the Russian regime, such articles were rare in the *Century* during the 1950s.

In American politics, they were critical of Harry S. Truman, beginning with his use of the atomic bomb. Maybe it did save lives, but the war could have been ended through other means. Japan, it was said, was ready in January 1945 with the very terms the United States accepted in August; why had we not agreed earlier? Why build resentment and Japan's will to revenge? Why not at least have demonstrated the A-bombs' power before dropping it on cities? Why not? Whoever might consider the magazine as naïve about science and progress would do well to turn to the editorial "Man and the Atom" (August 22, 1945). It took a sort of sorcerer's apprentice view of what science, under Truman's unleashing of negative atomic power, was doing and could do. Science was a threat, not a messiah. One week later there was "America's Atomic Atrocity," a theme for years of concern about responsibility, regulation and the like. "The atomic bomb can fairly be said to have struck Christianity itself."

So wary of Truman were the editors that some sort of wishful thinking must have left them ready for Thomas E.

Dewey in 1948. (I promised a howler.) *The Christian Century* was as caught as the *Chicago Tribune* with its premature headline announcing the Dewey victory. A week before the election the magazine had nominated Christian statesman John Foster Dulles as Dewey's secretary of state. Then on November 10, 1948, having gone to press just before the election, the *Century* advised President-elect Dewey on atomic control. The next issue had to open with "Whatever became of that President-elect? How wrong we were!" The magazine ate crow for several issues, as the letters to the editor show.

On the international scene, one major theme of these years was Zionism, focusing on the birth of Israel in 1948. The editors and most contributors did not support the state of Israel as created, or the way it was created. Frequently writers expressed regret over wartime policies toward refugees and immigrants, including those in the United States. There was constant and genuine concern for the Jews who survived the Holocaust. By now, however, the Reform Jews—with whom the editors had sympathized from Balfour Declaration times in 1918 to the prime of Hitler around 1938—were largely persuaded, for understandable reasons, by the political cause of Israel. So by 1948 they were no longer sources or allies for the editors. Thus the editors were reduced to magnifying pathetically small and marginal groups, like the American Council for Judaism and other vestigial anti-Zionist voices.

Yet editorials of those years foresaw clearly the forthcoming Arab-Israeli hostility. The *Century* did better than many in representing the valid cause of those displaced by the new state, but only very reluctantly did it come to terms with the reality of Israel.

W HEN THE EDITORS felt that they had to cover the emerging pluralism in this country, most frequently they reported on the "menace" of assertive Catholicism. In the January 21, 1948, issue they published the full "Manifesto by 'Protestants and Other Americans United' " for separation of church and state. POAU was the last coalition between liberal and conservative Protestants—Morrison, the editor, and Louis D. Newton, president of the Southern Baptist Convention, were two of the five signers, and middle-of-the-roader John A. Mackay of Princeton was typical of another part of the spectrum.

POAU intended to be vigilant about all excursions across the "wall of separation," and it often scored Protestant groups. It was occasioned, however, by fears that Catholicism was getting too large a piece of the pluralist pie. A celebrated series by future editor Harold E. Fey on "Can Catholicism Win America?" operated on an almost universal mainline Protestant assumption. Oversimplified, the belief was that if Catholic growth were sustained and reached 51 percent of the population—though a smaller figure could do—it would alter and dominate the country's institutions. Why? Because the Catholic Church was monolithic, united, authoritarian and mobilizable the way Protestant churches were not. The manifesto reads, along the way:

> A powerful church, unaccustomed in its own history and tradition to the American ideal of separation of church and state, but flourishing under the religious liberty provided by our [I am allowed one *sic*?] form of government, and emboldened by the wide diffusion of a false conception of tolerance, has committed itself in authoritative declarations and by positive acts to a policy plainly subversive of religious liberty as guaranteed by the Constitution.

It is hard to think one's way back to the times before Vatican II, before ecumenical and self-critical Catholicism, before non-Catholic awareness of intra-Catholic conflict and the like, to reconstruct a plausible basis for such understandings. Today intrusions or violations of "the wall" come as readily from aggressive Protestants as from Catholics. As things stood at mid-century, however, the "even-handed" POAU soon took on the image of an anti-Catholic group. Fifteen years later as the magazine became a leader in interpreting Vatican II Catholicism, it progressively distanced itself from the POAU heritage, but in 1949, Charles Clayton Morrison—retired as editor, but still a contributing editor—gave an article-length defense of POAU objectives (February 23). "This movement is not anti-Catholic in the sense of opposition to the Catholic Church, as such." But . . . And the Vatican ambassadorship issue arose again under Truman, provoking far,

far more editorial response than it deserved. At the same time, the editors stayed alert to positive signs in Catholic theology and social thought, even as they answered a fearful Yes when they asked, "Can Catholicism Win America?"

Given the public visibility and growth of the evangelical-pentecostal-fundamentalist Protestant sector in recent decades, it is interesting to see how marginal it looked to the mainstream up to 1952. It is instructive to monitor the coverage of the young evangelist Billy Graham, who received fairly neutral and certainly not wholly negative comment during these years.

In the news section of December 28, 1949, the Minneapolis correspondent began to introduce the name. "Who is he?" Minneapolitans were asking of Graham, fresh back from a sensational Los Angeles campaign, which the *Century*'s Los Angeles correspondent had failed to note at the time. This "blond, hard-hitting Southern Baptist preacher," handpicked to head the fundamentalist Northwestern Schools in St. Paul, remained an unknown. Gradually the editors began moving Graham toward the front pages, but they did not connect him with the large-scale revival of the evangelicalism that they thought ecumenical Christianity was leaving behind.

Today it is hard to re-create the sense of cultural space that mainline Protestantism occupied—and was gradually having to share with Catholics, Jews and conservative Protestants. Articles on "cults" were relatively rare during those fifteen years. "I Am" claimed a million members; Moral Re-Armament demanded watching. Yet if "center and periphery" and "mainstream and marginal" are blurred and confused today, the power of center and mainstream was unquestionable then. I do not think this was a mere illusion of power, though the editors were not past being blind to limits of their threatened world. The reporting, not the editorializing, confirms the power of the mainstream.

Picture today anything like the "America for Christ" banner across the October 19, 1949, issue. "The die is cast. American Protestantism is committed. On October 3, thirty-eight denominations set out to win as many as possible of the 70 million unchurched people of this country to a living evangelical faith." It was to be a fifteen-month "march against the pagan secularism, spiritual illiteracy and open unbelief of the

Poster introducing the young Billy Graham
BILLY GRAHAM CENTER

majority of our citizens." A variety of tested methods would be used widely in a United Evangelistic Advance by 35 million churchpeople. "It deserves to succeed. It must not fail."

81

One reads little in follow-up during those fifteen months. If the advance failed, that would "reveal that Protestantism has wasted its magnificent American heritage and is no longer the major spiritual force in the mature life of the nation it brought to birth, cradled in infancy and guided in youth." The editors saw this as an hour of decision for Protestant influence.

Why did the mainstream lose its will and strategic position? The *Century* pages give some clues.

Never overlook the power of nontheological factors. Let me half speculate and say that the fate of common Protestantism was much tied to "downtown"—downtown Seattle and Minneapolis and Kalamazoo. Downtown churches and ministers became prominent simply by being downtown. Then white Protestants would converge in rallies of thousands, whether for Reformation festivals or moral causes or morale-building celebrations. The suburban dispersal caused a loss of coherence and commonality, thus the decline of church federations and joint activities.

Add to this the gradual loss of enemies. Group coherence came from the fear of the Catholic or secularist menaces, and when the leadership turned ecumenical and open to God's activity beyond the walls of the churches, they sapped themselves of certain energies. Not that the editors felt Protestants had won or were winning the world, leaving no enemies out there. But the old bogeys were disappearing; Catholicism was changing, and Protestants who came to know Catholic neighbors lost their extreme negativism.

PROTESTANT THEOLOGY was in fairly good shape then. The major theologians of Euro-American neo-orthodoxies were not remote academics: Karl Barth preached in the prisons, and Reinhold Niebuhr was a circuit-rider. Theologians made *Time* covers and were publicly recognized, while they also kept credentials in the academy. One envies book review editors who could critique Baillie and Baillie and Berdyaev and Buber and Bultmann and Barth and Brunner and Bonhoeffer, and still have twenty-five other letters of the alphabet to review. One enjoys reading how the editors wrestled with the legacies of Alfred North Whitehead and John Dewey, who died in this period, or Albert Schweitzer, who visited America. Another decade's round of the "How My Mind Has Changed" series found the Europeans less remote than before from American concerns, and the Americans more alert to the critical theology of Europe. The editors had plenty of judgment calls to make, but they did enjoy the game.

At the same time, mainstream Protestantism, somewhat symbolized by Eisenhower's bland piety, had so blended with the woodwork of its America that it lost visibility, color and vitality. Judaism, familiar in suburb and on campus, was making new moves. Catholicism was becoming a regular partner and ally with non-Catholics on the civic, social and humanitarian scene; despite the aggressiveness of the Cardinal Spellmans, there were also cooperative sides. Billy Graham was making evangelism and evangelicalism visible. And a new vitality had come to secular thought in the postwar years.

All these advanced at the expense of mainstream Protestantism, which tried a bit to be mean, but meanness didn't stick. The editors found themselves developing "Plan B" for America. Whoever has read about religious change almost anywhere in the world has to be impressed how this shift occurred in America with no dead bodies, no (to my knowledge) physical wounds from intergroup squabbles, and fewer psychic scars than one could have expected. The retreat or yielding, in other words, was in part strategic, often principled—and editors of this magazine, who had much at stake in the shift, played a significant part in the move.

A review of these years finds the magazine involved in some historic causes, while continuing to neglect others. There were signals that the "racial revolution"—the civil rights cause—was dawning on the horizon. When the magazine noticed or stimulated it, it tended to side with the angels. Yet there was a general understress, even neglect, of this cause that white Protestant liberals were slow to champion.

The postwar years brought a few better signs on the "women" front. Margaret Frakes published a remarkable series that singled out prominent churchwomen, and occasional articles advocated enlarged roles for women in religious and national life. It would be dishonest to represent equality as a high-priority cause, however. The question of whether Catholic parochial-school children were to ride public school buses free of charge drew more ink and blood than the cause of justice for women or blacks. To recall the set of propositions that opened this article, one can make justifiable judgments here: Some people *were* advancing causes of racial minorities and women better than liberal Protestants or Christians in general. At least the editors did not retard the cause; they kept alive a consciousness that could quickly be vitalized when the change began to come. Then the magazine wrote happier chapters that stimulated such change.

Alfred Schutz has spoken about "imposed" and "intrinsic" relevance. World War II imposed on *The Christian Century* an agenda that the editors could not dodge. They reached into their resources and responded appropriately. In the years of peace that followed they found themselves "intrinsically" relevant, since many parts of their vision could now help shape a world. The editors were at home in a world that formed the United Nations and the National and World Councils of Churches. These agencies—always subject to the editors' severe criticism—at least embodied international and ecumenical ideals of moving beyond the tribalism that had killed and hurt so much.

Realism, more than is usually acknowledged, marked the writings of these editors. If events soon shattered their plans, and if latter-day celebrators of belligerance, tribalism and hardheadedness disdain some of their goals, this does not mean they have nothing to teach us. One can profit by re-examining their compromised positions, as on Israel, or their blind spots, as on Catholicism. But better lessons may lie in the consistency of their Christic concern, in their love for the republics of politics and letters, and in their wrestling with the problems of pluralism, as both menace and promise.

Theirs was hardly a starry-eyed optimism; they knew that struggles were inevitable in the future of the world, the country and the church. What sustained the editors through all the years was articulated at the very beginning of the postwar period in an August 22, 1945, editorial, "The Church's Responsibility." "The apocalyptic end of the war" lay upon the church a responsibility to "preach to modern man the good news of possible salvation." Faced with Catholic clericalism, Orthodox binding, European Protestant devastation, confrontations with old and new paganisms, the irrelevance of much of American Protestantism, and ominous signs that, by standards of human judgment, the church was unequal to its task, the editors relied on a secret for hope. "That secret is found not in its own strength but in the power which surges into the church again and again from its living head, the Lord Jesus Christ."

The Christian Century did not want to miss out on any seven days' worth of events or ideas related to that secret or its power and source. Readers got the point. ■

Integration and Imperialism: The *Century* 1953-1961

JAMES M. WALL

T HE HISTORY of *The Christian Century* moves at this
point into what we could call the "modern era." That
designation is relative since "modern" means recent, and recent covers more time for some of us than for others. But as
the current editor, I am exercising an administrative preroga-
tive by beginning the "modern" years in 1953—the year that
I first took seriously this weekly publication as it made its
regular appearance in my seminary library in Atlanta. And in
the same executive spirit, I am assuming that our centennial
history should conclude with 1971, the year before I was ap-
pointed editor.

It is possible that like so many undergraduate students I
had earlier run across the magazine in doing library research.
But it was not until I enrolled at Emory University's Candler
School of Theology that I recall regularly seeing this rather
foreboding periodical, whose cover each week notified readers
of four or five topics that awaited within. Having spent the
previous six years in various forms of journalism, my first
impression was that *The Christian Century* could use a design
artist. But my second impression was the one that stuck: Here
was world Christianity presented with a sophistication that
challenged the parochialism of my southern Methodism.

Mr. Wall is editor of The Christian Century.

These memories of my seminary years returned as I began reading through issues of the *Century* beginning with January 7, 1953. This chapter will cover the magazine through the end of 1961; the final chapter will begin with 1962 and conclude with 1971. We will leave it to our succeeding editors to evaluate the magazine's post-1972 efforts.

As 1953 began, Dwight D. Eisenhower moved into the White House. He was greeted warmly in the pages of the *Century* by editors who had earlier expressed some uneasiness over a military general's assuming the chief-executive role. Editorials were unsigned, so it is not possible to determine if they were written by Paul Hutchinson, then two-thirds through his nine-year stint as editor; or by executive editor Harold E. Fey, who was to follow Hutchinson in the top position in 1956; or by some other staff member. But one can assert that in the editorial section, "the *Century* said" was a legitimate description.

When Eisenhower came to Washington, the *Century* welcomed him with praise for both his stern anticommunism and his evident piety, two qualities that would characterize the magazine's attitude toward domestic and foreign affairs as well as religion and politics for some time to come. When the president was baptized and joined a Presbyterian church in Washington on confession of faith, the magazine saw this as an expression of a man who wanted Christian faith to affect his political life. By April the editors had become ecstatic about the new president, lauding his "magnificent" call for "a peace which is true and total" in Korea. Public expression of religious faith by a national leader was considered evidence of inner faith. There was no indication of cynicism, or any suspicion that religion might be used to curry public favor.

Throughout this Eisenhower era and into the 1960s, the editors reflected a liberal imperialism, best exemplified in public life by Adlai Stevenson. They believed that communism had to be stopped at every point, because American democracy was superior and was transferable to all parts of the world. The best way to propagate democracy was by example and through financial support, not by military might. Their resistance to communism, it should be noted, was still well to the left on the political spectrum. The shrillness of a Senator

Joseph McCarthy and the bluster and name-calling of the House Un-American Activities Committee were consistently attacked by the *Century*. When one subscriber wrote to accept a trial offer on the condition that the editor and his staff sign a pledge that none was "or ever had been" a member of the Communist Party, editor Hutchinson was so incensed that he didn't just return the money, but told of its return in a long editorial: "We are Christians, not Communists; . . . our understanding of what it means to be Christian makes it impossible for us to be Communist. . . . [But] we shall not sign this oath" (June 10, 1953).

That incident provides a capsule view of how liberals viewed the communist issue in the early 1950s. Democracy was superior, and one reason for that involved the right of any citizen to refuse to reveal his or her private political convictions. When Methodist Bishop G. Bromley Oxnam of Washington, D.C., voluntarily testified before the House Un-American Activities Committee, chaired by Harold Velde (R., Ill.), to clear himself of charges of disloyalty to the country, liberal Christians found a new hero.

On July 22, 1953, Oxnam appeared in a crowded congressional hearing room to demand that the Velde committee clean up its files and stop attacking Protestant clergy on flimsy charges, some of which the *Century* suspected were trumped up by the ultraconservative American Council of Churches. Oxnam later published his testimony and described his experience in the book *I Protest;* a *Century* advertisement for the book hailed Oxnam for turning "the hearing into a forum on elementary justice and civil rights."

The early part of the decade was a tense time, with Senator McCarthy making his reckless charges and the nation on edge after a war in Korea against communist North Korea and the People's Republic of China (often termed Red China, even in the *Century,* for most of the decade).

After an armistice was signed in the summer of 1953 the *Century* indicated its support of the United Nations action in Korea by asserting that "now that aggression has been restrained at great cost in life and material, it is to be hoped that communist expansionists have been taught a lesson and that

89

Methodist bishop G. Bromley Oxnam (1891–1963)
METHODIST INFORMATION SERVICES

no other test of like character will be demanded of United Nations members" (August 5).

THE LIBERAL-CONSERVATIVE division in American political life was to become sharply sectional through the rest of the decade after the Supreme Court's 1954 decision outlawing segregation in public schools, a traumatic moment in American history that the *Century* began to anticipate months

90

before the decision itself. Despite its image as a northern liberal journal, the *Century* was patient toward the southern states—an attitude that probably had more to do with liberal optimism than with political realism. One author predicted before the ruling that segregation would be outlawed and that the way to make a reasonable transition into integrated education would be to start with first-grade children and allow the process to be completed over a twelve-year period.

The court decision to "postpone for months hearings on the means and time-schedule by which school segregation is to be abolished" was greeted warmly by the *Century,* whose editors predicted that "this ruling will be calmly received in the south and . . . public opinion will swing behind efforts to give it honest implementation" (June 2). The editors added: "A great deal of what might be called the silent public opinion of the south has already marked off segregation as a doomed and dying social arrangement."

Unfortunately, as the magazine discovered through the next decade, that silent opinion, although present, was slow to make itself heard in public policy. Six years later, as numerous editorials and articles indicate, the Methodist church—then the largest Protestant body in the nation, with heavy southern concentration—was still struggling to resolve its own institutional segregation. Its Central Jurisdiction, formed as a separate structure for black churches, was still in place, setting a bad example for public schools.

Martin Luther King, Jr., entered the *Century* pages for the first time in March 1956 when Harold Fey chronicled the boycott of the bus system in Montgomery, Alabama, and King's arrest in connection with it. By the end of the decade King had become the recognized civil rights leader and frequently wrote for—or was quoted in—the magazine. Later he became an editor-at-large. The *Century,* in 1963, was the first nationally distributed periodical to publish his famous "Letter from Birmingham Jail" in its entirety.

In 1958, as the *Century* celebrated its fiftieth anniversary since its "refounding" in 1908 when Charles Clayton Morrison took over the fledgling periodical, James P. Wesberry, one of a large number of correspondents who regularly filed news accounts from around the world, reported that an Atlanta,

Martin Luther King, Jr. (1929–1968)
RELIGIOUS NEWS SERVICE PHOTO

Georgia, pastor denounced his fellow Georgians' silence on the integration issue. Roy O. McClain of Atlanta's First Baptist Church employed his prestigious platform to confess courageously that "college professors have been relatively quiet on the race issue, the pulpits have been paralyzed and the politicians are interested in getting votes." The truth is, he charged, the South "doesn't have a voice because the well-informed people have been quiet" (January 29).

In his report, Wesberry illustrated what the only public

noises from the South were like. Georgia Governor Marvin Griffin had responded to people wondering what would happen to federal lunchroom funds if the state refused to integrate its schools with the assertion: "I'm gonna tell [government officials] to get up their blackeyed peas, get up their taters, get up their stew pots, and get out of here. We can feed our children ourselves." Wesberry concluded his report: "So goes the story of segregation and integration in this part of the world."

As a pastor in that "part of the world" during this decade, I well remember those lonely voices amid the silence of public opinion. They were reassuring and gave the rest of us some hope that the future would be better. But we also knew that we were a long way from achieving the normal integrated patterns that the *Century* had hopefully predicted in 1954.

ECUMENISM, long a concern of the magazine, flourished in the fifties, beginning with the high excitement before, during and after the World Council of Churches Assembly in Evanston, Illinois, in the summer of 1954. The magazine noticed little else during the period of the meeting—partly a reflection of the geographical nearness of the event itself (a mere short train ride away), and partly because the 1947 Amsterdam Assembly—following as it did upon the end of World War II—had been relatively subdued.

Evanston was to be exciting. The Assembly opened with rousing addresses by an American and a German, both stressing the theme, Christian hope. An indication of the enthusiasm generated by the gathering of world Christians can be seen in the closing session at Chicago's Soldier Field, where more than 125,000 people gathered to celebrate, worship and prepare for another seven years of service and theologizing. Reporting on the meeting, the *Century* concluded that too much of the Assembly's time was spent in theological disputes. What saved the meeting—ironically, in contrast to later developments—was the agreement on social action. "Could it be that if the World Council studied its theology less dogmatically and more in action from the saddle, so to speak, that the council would last longer and go farther?" the editors asked. Generally acclaimed, however, was the Assembly's recognition

*WCC officials at Soldier Field, Chicago, in 1954. Left to right, they
are Dr. W. A. Visser't Hooft, Dr. Marc Boegner,
Bishop G. Bromley Oxnam, Archbishop Athenagoras,
Bishop B. K. A. Bell, and Bishop Eivind Berggrav.*
RELIGIOUS NEWS SERVICE PHOTO

of the two emerging continents, Asia and Africa, which could
no longer be dismissed as a "colorful geographical fringe."

Acquiring its new name of the "Christian" century in
1900, the magazine still held out hopes that the world could
be Christianized, fostering the same imperialistic evangelism
that had characterized Protestant mission effort for fifty years.

Evanston was provided once again with a formidable list of the
obstacles in the pathway of a Christian *occupation* [italics added]
of these two continents, and we would not minimize them.
The power of religious nationalism, the revival of the ancient
faiths, the hard shell of a social culture which cannot be pen-
etrated by the arrival of "another religion" or by attempts to
replace something old with something new—we know these

Official emblem of the NCC, 1955
NATIONAL COUNCIL OF CHURCHES

barricades are there. What we missed at Evanston was a call to move up into the breaches, to storm the citadels [September 22, 1954].

Earlier in the decade *Century* editors had reflected their Midwestern parochialism—and their prescience—in evaluating the emergence of the National Council of Churches as a major factor in American religious life. Commenting on the NCC's first assembly meeting in Denver, Colorado, in late 1952, Charles Clayton Morrison, then a contributing editor, defended the council as an "artifact, which does not belong to the nature of the church," but which nevertheless deserved support from denominations as a vehicle for moving away from the divisions within the church caused by "human contrivances" (January 7, 1953). Separateness was a sin "for which we pray to be forgiven" whenever ecumenical gatherings are

95

held, he asserted. In this separateness, the newly formed council "represents the most comprehensive effort American Protestantism has yet made to return from its wanderings in the wilderness of sectarianism and find its home in the true Church of Christ."

Morrison feared that denominational hubris would work against the new council. Soon after that, the editors saw danger for the NCC on another front: the proposed location of the NCC headquarters in New York City. Arguing against New York as the site, the editors pointed out that

> New York's Protestant population is only one-tenth as numerous as its combined Catholic and Jewish populations. This one factor should weigh decisively against choosing that city as the nation's center of Protestant life. Numerical insignificance inevitably invests Protestant church life with a minority mentality [May 12, 1954].

This situation, the editors maintained, would carry over into staff and leadership attitudes and "blight the realization of the Protestant mission in this land."

New York's "alien and demoralizing environment" was simply not conducive to a majority religion's performing its proper function. Columbus, Chicago and St. Louis were all proposed by the editors as cities within the heartland of Protestant strength. That attitude reflects the strong Protestant-first mind-set of the magazine, which was to play such a strong role in the closing years of this decade when a Roman Catholic presented himself as a candidate for the presidency of the United States.

THE LIKELIHOOD of a Catholic president at first appeared ominous to the magazine editors, who, in early 1959, warned against the possible influence of the "hierarchy of the Roman Catholic Church." Tracing the interest of the bishops of the Catholic Church in obtaining federal monies for parochial schools, the magazine recalled that the church leaders had sought to obtain funding and avoid the "impending danger of a judicial establishment of secularism that would ban God from public life." In response to this warning, the editors pointed out that our laws do not "ban God from public life," but they do ban the bishops from "the public treasury" (March 4, 1959). Clearly, the *Century* was concerned about a church hierarchy that it felt was not sensitive to "the pluralism essential for the separation of church and state."

As the 1960 campaign opened, a *Century* editorial reported that John F. Kennedy had once turned down an invitation to dedicate a Baptist chapel because his church disapproved of his entering a non-Roman Catholic sanctuary. The presidential candidate told the press that he had in fact declined such an invitation nine years earlier, explaining that he had been invited to represent his church, and since his church could not recognize the validity of the church involved, he had to decline. The *Century* noted that similar invitations might arise were he to be elected president.

In a two-part series examining "religion and the presidency" Robert S. Michaelsen, then a professor at the State University of Iowa in Iowa City, concluded that in time a non-Protestant might be elected, but not in "the near future," since the American people seem to desire "an embodiment of themselves" in the White House. Obviously, a Roman Catholic represented something other than mainstream America, so he could not "embody" the public.

Following Kennedy's nomination, Protestants formed groups to resist his election. Norman Vincent Peale was at first involved in one such group, but soon withdrew, declaring that he did not believe religion should be a factor in anyone's voting decision. In September, a few weeks before the election, Kennedy appeared before the Ministerial Association of Houston, Texas. His assertions that he was "against unconstitutional aid to parochial schools" and that "I do not speak for my church on public matters and the church does not speak for me" were enough to convince the *Century* that his election did not pose a serious threat to the sacred wall of separation. His statement in Houston, an editorial declared, "strengthens the evidence that Senator Kennedy could resist political pressure from his church" (September 28).

After Kennedy's victory, a young *Century* associate editor, Martin E. Marty, summed up the election in a fashion that was to become his trademark for decades to come. Displaying his gift of cogent insight and summary observation,

Marty observed that Kennedy's inauguration symbolically marked the end of Protestantism as a national religion and its advent as the "distinctive faith of a creative minority."

That "distinctive faith" ventured down a different ecumenical path in 1960 with the proposal by United Presbyterian Eugene Carson Blake that four major denominations—his own, the Methodist Church, the Episcopal Church and the United Church of Christ—merge into one denomination. His proposal, made in San Francisco just before a National Council assembly, was quickly seconded by Episcopal Bishop James Pike, and the idea was dubbed the Blake-Pike proposal. From it grew the Consultation on Church Union, which, twenty-four years later, continues to move toward some form of uniting with less verve than at the start, but still reflecting some hope for overcoming the Protestant divisions that prompted the original proposal.

Strongly affirming the idea of a united church, the *Century* praised the potential and then turned its attention to the next World Council of Churches Assembly, this time in far-off New Delhi, India. Perhaps the world ecumenical mood had dampened a bit, or perhaps the great distance had an impact. Whatever the reason, New Delhi did not evoke the excitement that had surrounded the 1954 Evanston Assembly. Organized ecumenism was clearly in a muted stage. Nonetheless, the editors were unceasing in their support of ecumenical organizations. In an earlier editorial, they had strongly affirmed the National Council's increasing tendency to issue proclamations and resolutions on social issues. Quoting a denominational paper's editorial, the *Century* said: "If anxious Protestants would actually read and digest the documents of the National Council . . . they would come to admire rather than to suspect this bulwark of Christian Protestantism in America" (July 12, 1961).

INTERNALLY, PROTESTANTISM had divisions in addition to denominational ones. The popularity of the dynamic young evangelist Billy Graham at first drew news coverage and then, as his ministry grew, brought sharp negative criticism. In a November 11, 1956, editorial, the editors wondered why Dr. Graham did not respond to public criticism from theologian Reinhold Niebuhr for not addressing "the race issue" in his preaching. It was not enough, the magazine observed, for Graham to write in a *Life* magazine article that "discrimination on the basis of race was unkind, [but] that Negroes should cultivate the virtue of patience." Graham ignored both Niebuhr and the *Century*.

Norman Vincent Peale's "positive thinking" was also harshly criticized in editorials and articles throughout the decade. But it was within the *Century*'s own family of authors that a particularly strong exchange occurred the next year. Reinhold Niebuhr on several occasions demanded that his German colleague Karl Barth be more forthcoming in opposing Soviet aggression in Eastern Europe. Following the 1956 Hungarian uprising, Niebuhr wrote a stinging rebuke of Barth, asking, "Why Is Barth Silent on Hungary?" The American writer observed that "even the lowly party hacks in the Communist parties of Britain and France have been shocked but Barth himself has remained silent" (January 23, 1957).

And when Barth published a letter he had written to an East German pastor, counseling him to be neutral toward the communist government there, Niebuhr was harsh in his objection to Barth's "above-the-battle Christian witness." Barth had told the pastor that loyalty to a state does not mean "regarding the state as good or agreeing with its purpose." To Niebuhr, however, it was necessary for Christians to "take our moral responsibilities in this world seriously and [that requires] hazardous political judgments" (February 11, 1959).

This mood of anticommunism among American liberals made it difficult for the *Century* to engender much support for Cuba's emerging revolution. Still, several long articles, including one by managing editor Theodore A. Gill, encouraged the United States to affirm the new government in that island as a welcome change from the oppression of Fulgencio Batista. Radicals of any stripe, however, were viewed with caution by the *Century*. For example, editor Harold Fey disliked Chicago social activist Saul Alinsky's confrontational methods of neighborhood organizing. The editors were still convinced that orderly and voluntary reform was the only method of social change that Christians should wholeheartedly support.

Almost as though in preparation for the coming civil rights struggle of the sixties, an American Baptist minister originally from South Carolina, Kyle Haselden, was named managing editor in 1960. He was to become recognized as a perceptive observer of the racial developments of the 1960s, a time when Martin Luther King's patient march toward equality began to give way to more violent methods of direct confrontation. Haselden would become editor in 1964, succeeding Harold Fey, who had taken over from Paul Hutchinson in January 1956. Three months after leaving the magazine, Hutchinson died of a heart attack while on a trip with his wife in Texas. Fey is still a *Century* contributing editor.

When the decade closed, a longtime fixture at the *Century* also closed his career. Halford Luccock, whose column had long appeared under the byline of Simeon Stylites, died at the age of seventy-five on November 5, 1960. He had begun his column as a "letter to the editor" in 1948, and it continued until just before his death. The column was a word of wisdom delivered with a touch of humor, and a gentle reminder of the human spirit's foibles.

One of Luccock's best was a 1954 column mourning the passing of the old tradition of Friday afternoon school poetry recitals. No longer, he lamented, did the assembly hall ring with the likes of "The Charge of the Light Brigade" or "Curfew Shall Not Ring Tonight."

> Today's sophisticates may say "how terribly quaint." It was more than quaint. It was storing the mind with music and imagination. People who learned to repeat poetry often kept it in mind for a lifetime. When a person does not know any poetry there is a dimension of mind and soul missing; part of the human heritage has been lost. . . . The Bible is [also] not in the memory of the multitudes. They do not possess its cadence or recognize its words. Few pastors would dare start to lead a congregation in repeating the First Psalm. Even the 23rd is a big risk. Half the congregation will still be feeding in green pastures while the more venturesome sheep have jumped on to eating at a table in the presence of their enemies [October 6].

That was Luccock's way of gently telling us that the olden times had much to contribute. We are the poorer for letting such practices get away from us. Which suggests again the value of looking back on our history. Much is there that tells us of the future. ■

Adopting Realism:
The *Century* 1962-1971

JAMES M. WALL

"*N*ACH AMERIKA *gehen? Das ist für Brunner, aber nicht für mich!*" *The Christian Century* quoted that statement (which may be apocryphal) from Karl Barth in preparing its readers for the eminent Swiss theologian's 1962 visit to the United States. Barth and the *Century* had viewed the world quite differently during the previous thirty-five years, a contrast the magazine oversimplified as withdrawal from the world to regroup (in Barth's case) versus continued involvement in society's struggles.

Then in April 1962, the seventy-year-old Barth lifted his boycott of the United States to accept a three-city invitation to deliver lectures in this country. His first stop was Chicago, where he packed the 2,400-seat Rockefeller Chapel at the University of Chicago for a series of talks titled "Introduction to Evangelical Theology." Seated in a front press pew just below the pulpit, the *Century* editors—long a journalistic embodiment of classic liberalism—came to debate (and to admire) this gracious man whose "pessimism" had so riled the optimistic American church. The editors were not converted in that weeklong exposure, but they were impressed with this man who had once likened the "American way of life" to the biblical "fleshpots of Egypt."

Eager to wage war against society's failure to care for the helpless, the *Century* had been restless with Barth's insistence that the church's prime responsibility was to open itself to

101

Karl Barth on his arrival in America, April 1962,
en route to the University of Chicago. RELIGIOUS NEWS SERVICE PHOTO

God's mysterious transcendence. Now, listening to him along with the worshipful and the skeptical, the editors had to acknowledge that "theology has come to be taken most seriously again in our time where it defines itself most modestly, without slippery movements into all the other disciplines, without fastening an encroaching grasp or a suffocating embrace on other human enterprises" (May 16, 1962).

It was a time, they understood Barth to be saying, to retreat in order to advance, prophesy, attack. But how could the church make that crucial move? Barth himself had "redefined theology" and put it to work with such passion that "no area of culture or society is really foreign to his interests." They noted that this Swiss scholar moved easily from Moses to Mozart, from Mesopotamia to East Germany, from obedience to Caesar to defiance of Hitler. However, even as they admired his catholicity, they still could not find the point at which the shift from transcendence to involvement took place.

There was no hostility in the *Century*'s coverage of Barth's American tour, only grudging admiration for the enormous impact of Barthian thought on every generation since the 1920s. And that influence touched the orthodox evangelical as readily as it reached the elite intellectual liberal.

Barth's visit became a media event in 1962, assured by his appearance on the cover of *Time*. But for the *Century* it marked something else: a slowly shifting awareness that, hereafter, social gains would be achieved in a more "realistic" atmosphere. The 1954 Supreme Court decision to integrate public schools "with all deliberate speed" was taking longer than the magazine had predicted. And a major obstacle to breaking the barriers of race was the church itself. The Methodists, for instance, were still mired in debate over what to do with their own segregated Central Jurisdiction. While Karl Barth's April 1962 visit did not break new theological ground, it did symbolize a fusion of optimism on this side of the Atlantic with Europe's doctrinal insistence that God would not be mocked by the slowness of society's structural changes.

The decade 1962-1971—the era covered by this final chapter in the *Century*'s centennial history—began with Barth's arrival and ended with the last gasp of the McGovern movement's political attempt to impose idealism on an increasingly conservative public.

In those years the *Century* and the rest of the country lived through three assassinations of national leaders—two Kennedy brothers and Martin Luther King, Jr. The war in Vietnam escalated to an appalling level, and racism became more ugly and obvious, not just an embarrassing presence in society. Three editors served the magazine in that period, an unusually frequent change of command for a magazine that has known only six chief editors from 1908 to the present.

In 1964 Harold E. Fey completed his twenty-four-year stint with the magazine—eight years as editor—just in time for former managing editor Kyle Haselden to begin his four-year editorship with an editorial endorsing President Lyndon B. Johnson for re-election. A brain tumor took Haselden's life at age fifty-five in 1968. He was succeeded by Alan Geyer, who served through 1971. I started my tenure in June of 1972.

The sixties were exhilarating times, stunning in sudden shifts of public sentiment and horrifying in the destruction from riots and war. Through the decade the *Century* kept a

Abraham Heschel, Henry Steele Commager, Martin Luther King, Jr.,
and John C. Bennett at a meeting of Clergy and Laymen Concerned
about Vietnam at Riverside Church in New York in April 1967
RELIGIOUS NEWS SERVICE PHOTO

watchful eye on some of its major concerns—race relations; church-state separation; the ongoing and welcome developments of Vatican II; the rights of the Palestinians; the threat of extremists to religious liberalism—but it displayed a realistic adjustment to the times. The imperialism that had led the editors to share cold-war sentiments against any manifestation of communist strength now gave way to a recognition that something other than communist expansionism was happening in Vietnam. The legitimate urge of a people to establish their own future was also at work.

In an impassioned report written from Washington, D.C., editor Haselden described a gathering of 2,400 clergy, seminarians, nuns and laypeople who came together January 31–February 1, 1967, "to condemn as morally irresponsible

U.S. military intervention in Vietnam's civil war, to plead with the administration to abandon brutal warfare against civilians and to beg their senators and representatives to take whatever steps are necessary to secure a negotiated peace" (February 15, 1967). The mobilization had been called by Clergy and Laymen Concerned About Vietnam, one of the first such efforts by the activist group now known as Clergy and Laity Concerned.

Haselden joined the conference's Illinois delegation when it visited its elected public servants. He was struck by the contrast between veteran Senator Everett Dirksen—who shouted at one delegate a "peevish, boorish command, 'Hush up!' "—and the state's freshman senator, Charles Percy—who displayed "an obvious willingness to have members of his constituency reason with him about [his stand]."

The two-day meeting also included two mass meetings at New York Avenue Presbyterian Church in Washington, featuring addresses by Robert McAfee Brown, William Sloane Coffin and Rabbi Abraham J. Heschel, each of whom would, in the ensuing years, continue to be outspoken opponents of the nation's Vietnam policy. Congressional support for the protesters ranged from the polite Percy audience to speeches from vigorous antiadministration senators: Wayne Morse (D., Ore.), Ernest Gruening (D., Alaska) and Eugene McCarthy (D., Minn.).

Rabbi Heschel twice quoted a section of a position paper by the event's organizers that stated the need to take steps for peace. "If we do not take those steps, we firmly believe that God will judge us harshly, and will hold us accountable for the horror we continue to unleash." The war in Vietnam, started under John F. Kennedy, was now being escalated into a major conflict by a president whom *The Christian Century* had endorsed just two and one-half years earlier.

THAT ENDORSEMENT broke with tradition, and it also cost the magazine a year's punishment by the Internal Revenue Service. The federal agency revoked the magazine's tax-exempt status for violating a specific regulation that forbids organizations covered by section 501-c-3 of the IRS code from endorsing political candidates. The rash step was taken early in the 1964 campaign with a lead editorial, "Johnson? Yes!" published September 9. Fey had stepped down as editor three weeks earlier, and, in one of his first editorials as the new editor, Haselden told readers that he was dropping "the other shoe," since Fey had written a "Goldwater? No!" editorial just before the Republican convention in July.

"Yes," Haselden boldly proclaimed, "we endorse Johnson." He did so not merely because of the fears raised by Goldwater, "but because a Johnson-Humphrey administration will handle both the perils and the promises facing this nation soberly, wisely and successfully." Johnson's "spotty" civil rights record caused some concern, but not enough to halt the endorsement.

Haselden was not naïve. He knew the IRS regulations as well as any other editor, but he dropped the "other shoe" because he strongly feared a Goldwater administration. Ironically, the technical violation of IRS rules might have gone unnoticed except that right-wing leader Billy James Hargis, who lost his tax exemption for politicizing his religious radio station, protested that the *Century*'s editorial exceeded the tax guidelines. An audit followed, after which the one-year punishment was leveled.

When Haselden in early 1967 joined church resistance to the Johnson administration's Vietnam policies, he was not being inconsistent with the 1964 endorsement. There had been a general consensus during the election that Johnson was to be trusted over Goldwater to keep his finger off the nuclear button. In congress the Gulf of Tonkin resolution, which gave the president unlimited freedom to pursue his war, passed with minimum protest. Soon, however, the optimism of 1964 vanished in the muddy jungles of Vietnam and the bloody streets of Saigon.

And as that optimism diminished, the *Century* also turned from its traditional assumption that American-style democracy was so superior to any other political option that it deserved automatic celebration wherever it encountered opposition. Right-wing extremists took over unbridled patriotism in the 1960s—a development that led, unfortunately, to the identification of the left, including the *Century,* as opponents of the United States. This identification, as the 1984 presidential campaign showed, allowed both sophisticated conservatives and anti-intellectual fundamentalists to brand any criticism of U.S. foreign policy as unpatriotic.

A good example of these false charges took place when, in 1962, John Bennett, then dean of Union Theological Seminary in New York City, submitted a letter to the editor in response to conservative attacks. Bennett had appeared on a television program and made the case that, as he explained it, "we should avoid identifying the Christian opposition to communism as a faith and an ideology with the international conflict involved in the 'cold war.' Christians should oppose communism by appropriate methods both religiously and politically, but they should not combine the passions of religion with the hostilities and fears of politics" (February 28, 1962).

Bennett was writing in reply to a charge in a newspaper column by Barry Goldwater, then two years away from his unsuccessful race for president. Goldwater, alluding to Bennett's TV appearance, quoted the theologian as saying that "the church should not fight communism." Bennett pointed out in his letter that Goldwater omitted an important adjective in that quote, for he had actually argued that the church should not be engaged in "a *holy war* against communism."

The issue joined between Bennett and Goldwater in 1962 is precisely the same battle that is being waged in the eighties, and the right's tactics do not seem to have changed—though its sophistication has increased. Indeed, in the 1960s the liberal church leadership grew careless in part because the opposition from the right was so bombastic and uninformed. Carl McIntire's crusade was in full force then, but he attracted little serious public attention. Fred Schwarz's Christian Anti-Communism Crusade became something of a traveling road show, moving into major cities to preach patriotism and hatred, denouncing the "commie-led World Council of Churches."

One of Schwarz's crusades took place in Seattle, Washington. Just before the crusade, Protestant, Catholic and Jewish leaders in the city issued a strong statement denouncing those "who cast doubt upon the loyalty of the state department and officials in other departments of government, and many of our proven patriots and statesmen of long standing" (February 28, 1962). The Seattle leaders insisted that they "stood adamant against the communist evil," but they wanted the public to notice the "threatening likeness between certain anticommunist movements now in vogue and events which transpired in Germany and Italy incident to the rise of the nazi and fascist regimes."

THE EARLY sixties, then, were a time when liberals fought against extremism from the right, even as they constantly repeated their abhorrence of communism. By the end of the decade, however, as the McGovern crusade caught on and seized the imagination of the young, abhorrence of communism gave way in some cases to grudging admiration and, in extreme cases, outright endorsement. In contrast, there had been no Jane Fondas in the early sixties to goad the nation's conservatives.

What we did have throughout that decade, as the *Century* pages indicate, was a growing dismay over the inability of a democracy to halt racism at home and an immoral war abroad. As they despaired over fostering change through the process, secular antiwar movements—which strongly influenced church attitudes, both negatively and positively—became extreme in their efforts to awaken a stubborn public. Long-haired youth brandishing Vietnamese flags and the sight of an American flag being burned and trampled soon turned the national mood from unease to ugliness. Polarization took over, and by the time the Democratic Party (with the almost unanimous support of mainline liberal churchpeople) had reformed itself enough to take the presidential nomination from traditional liberals and bestow it on a more radical candidate, the crusade's tactics had doomed the movement to minority status.

If one looks back from the perspective of the 1984 Reagan landslide, it is evident that the defeat of radicalism in 1972 has now been joined in history by the defeat of traditional liberalism in 1984. First McGovern and later Mondale, both sons of Methodist preachers, were decisively repudiated by the American public. That repudiation, however, need not be the final word on the turmoil of the 1960s, a time when change was not, in fact, slow, and did not come with "deliberate speed" but was harshly thrust upon us. Progress was made then through a liberal religious-secular alliance.

Today in the 1980s a potential war in Nicaragua draws widespread opposition, military budgets are closely examined, and social programs are still defended. Victories don't always come through political elections; sometimes, as has been said of John Ford movies, we may achieve "victory through defeat."

This may be an insight gained from merging the pessimism that Karl Barth felt about humankind and the optimism he felt about the transcendent God—insight that came gradually to *The Christian Century* editors during the 1960s. ■

The End of a Century, The Beginning of a Century

MARTIN E. MARTY

MODESTY forced the breaking off of *The Christian Century* story more than a dozen years before the end of its first century. Had they traced the magazine's history to 1984—its actual centennial—the editor, the managing editor, and the other senior editor, my coauthors of this book, would have had to appraise their own achievements. As a thirty-year *Century* veteran, I am the staff member with the longest tenure. I have known five of the magazine's six directing editors and served under four, and as a professional historian, I am assumed to have a perspective from which an updating and evaluation of the journal's more recent history can occur with less risk of the charge of bias.

From the angles of vision provided by four decades of reading and three of writing for this magazine, I am able to perceive vast changes. These unfold week by week, as the editors write obituaries for some lost causes, encomia for occasional winners, and appraisals of a world too complex to be reduced to losings and winnings. Let me single out a few changes that have been advanced during the present editorial administration. Some of these have come about as the result of Acts of Editors, people who shape a world. Others are responses to Acts of God, changes in a world they do not and cannot shape and that their weekly words can only address.

One vast area of development has to do with editorial

responsibility toward ecumenical constituencies and with a growing vision of ecumenical reality. Originally, *The Christian Century* had been denominational, belonging to the family of the Disciples of Christ, a group that had not wanted to be denominational in the first place. Then the magazine became rather militantly undenominational for many decades. Its editors were friendly to and gave space to Reform Jews and had occasional words of praise for individual Roman Catholics. Yet the magazine's profile was Christian, Protestant, anti-Catholic, and, when controversy heated, antifundamentalist in such a sweeping way that whatever was not what today is called "mainline" was seen as fundamentalist. "Minority," sectarian, and nonmainline WASP religion in general was regarded as marginal, eccentric, and sometimes malign.

Change has been drastic. While no editors could hope to satisfy all interests in the Middle East—the obvious Jewish ones, well spoken up for by Jews and Christians in America, or the competing putatively "pro-Arab" or "even-handed" alternatives supported by some American Christians—overall, Jews have regarded the magazine as fair and friendly both to them and to Israel. Second, Roman Catholicism now is reported on and judged on the same terms as the rest of Christianity. It is clearly seen as part of "our" faith and house. There has also been a great deal of discrimination concerning reactionary Protestantisms. While militant and obscurantist fundamentalism rarely gets a friendly hearing in the journal's pages, mind-their-business fundamentalists draw respect. Even more, the moderate parties called evangelical are not permitted to stand off or to be stood off. Their authors are at home on these pages; their members make up large parts of our readership.

In *The Public Church: Mainline-Evangelical-Catholic* (Crossroad, 1981), I argued that a new "coalescence," not a new organization, was emerging. The plot of that book squares with my observation of how this magazine has viewed the ecumenical scene. In brief, certain kinds of mainline Protestants, evangelicals, and Roman Catholics have more in common with each other—and know it and show it—than they do with others in their own nominal camps. They have developed a "public theology" that allows them to be faithful to their own creeds and callings while opening up in new ways to common thought and action across boundaries.

Such change has brought some problems and chaos to the formal—in Max Weber's sense "routinized"—ecumenical movement. The magazine continues to monitor, criticize, and support this movement as it goes through a "period of adjustment." The *Century* has rued the times when ecumenical councils have been misrepresented, judged them when they badly represented themselves and their causes, and cheered them on in tasks of revision. Though the ecumenical movement has often been in trouble, the editors have found the ecumenical spirit to be durable, often hearty.

On another front the magazine has recognized some failures, both in the church and in its own coverage. During the fifteen years since the previous installment of the story left off, the Christian majority and the statistical balance of power have shifted to the southern part of the globe. The magazine has eagerly reported on accompanying stresses and distresses and has applauded efforts at sympathy and empathy across North/South, rich/poor boundaries. Yet budgetary constraints have limited its news coverage of the physically faraway but now so spiritually near scene. Were a generous foundation to endow the *Century* and liberate it to fulfill its mission and vision, most funds would go into more extensive coverage of African, Latin American, Asian, and even European worlds.

Closer to home, while the magazine pioneered in American journalism in promoting and reporting on women in religion and, under Kyle Haselden and even some of his predecessors, gained a reputation for civil rights advocacy and reportage of the black and minority churches, there now is cause for disappointment on these scores. After the death of Martin Luther King, Jr., the black and white churches seemed to put a lower priority on common awareness, action, and life. We have not done enough to report on the black and Hispanic churches, or to discern or develop writing and editorial talent among them. The new century demands more of the magazine on this front.

In addition to these changes, the style of the *Century*'s editorial mission has taken a new direction. The magazine was born and thrived as "advocacy journalism." Its editors always wanted to be fair, but they also wanted to be partisan and interesting. For many decades, the journal was the rallying point for many liberal causes. But today the lines within the worlds of theology, politics, economics, and the arts are less clearly drawn. Some would say that their complexity is chaotic. The world the editors keep referring to as "pluralistic" is not one in which the good girls/guys are so easily separated from the bad. (I do believe that an objective difference can be noted and depicted between the mean and the nonmean, but I probably could not sell such a discernment of spirits to the editors or readers.)

Much of the talk about "conservative" and "liberal" spreads more confusion than clarity, and recent editors have generally backed off from such neat stereotyping. Not that there is less of it around! Indeed, many who found us too conservative fifteen years ago, after their own 180-degree changes, now find us too liberal or radical—even where it is only they, not we, who have significantly changed. (If people have headed in the other direction these years, we have not heard about it; conservative chic has been "in" during the years since editor Wall left off the story a chapter ago.)

Not in order to win favor, votes, or subscriptions from people who do not belong to the old *Century* party, but out of editorial conviction, the magazine has altered its posture. No more ready to be dull than were their predecessors, the editors believe that in the current dispensation they can at the same time be interesting and non- or bipartisan, opening the pages to competing voices. Sometimes the editors may represent such voices among themselves. There is less overt advocacy. There is more interest in shades of gray, discriminations, scrupulous judgments, and applications of the ironic eye to all endeavors—including the editors' own. "Knee-jerk" is a dirty word that will help kill editorials or submitted articles.

In this respect, the editors do not feel that they are being trendy. The national trend has been to draw ever more sharply the lines of East/West and other struggles, as if there were not naturally enough line drawing and as if religious, indeed Christian, writing had to add emotional fire to what was already burning hot. The magazine has found its voice and even prospered by seeing to it that it has *not* been able to be dismissed as predictable. Ideologues of right and left might accuse it of being so, and there may be lapses. Yet the intention and ideal is to include surprises, third angles on polarized causes and stories, some unpredictability—but not, one hopes, simple inconsistency.

Editor Wall says that the theology of Reinhold Niebuhr informs much of what goes on in the magazine's pages. In some ways, this should be no surprise, since Niebuhr was a "discovery" of the *Century*'s editors, who gave him early encouragement in the 1920s. Though they broke radically with him as World War II neared, they and he came to convergence on many issues in the later years of his life. One must not make too much of this association, since the Niebuhrian nose can be twisted by so many ideologues to match their ideologies. Yet it is an effort by Wall and his contemporaries to say something about the stance with which they would like to see this example of religious journalism help usher in its second century and, soon, see the Third Millennium C.E. unfold.

Rather than quote Niebuhr to define the approach in question, let me draw on political scientist Elie Kedourie, in his *The Crossman Confessions and Other Essays in Politics, History and Religion* (Mansell, 1984). Those who write in this spirit see as examplars

> prophets [who] maintain a distance from current political arrangements, and deal with power at arm's length: the attitude they articulate is that the body politic, a human contrivance and thus necessarily subject to decay and failure, is not that which gives meaning and coherence to human life. On the contrary, politics is perpetually under judgment, God's judgment revealed through prophets.

Emphatically, such an observation has not made this magazine's editors into prophets, sons and daughters of prophets, or would-be prophets. They are critics, who feel free to criticize, seek justice, and announce judgments from time to time. They are also compromised humans who have a zest for the modest yet immeasurably great gifts of God on which they do report: politics, the arts, the life of the churches, the expressions of the human spirit. They intend to continue their pursuits vigorously.

In this book current editors appraise and hold up for

A Century of the *Century*

appraisal the work of their predecessors. Weekly, in the century to come, they will be holding up their own, for new generations to read, criticize and, they hope, be surprised by. ∎

116